INDIE AUTHOR MAGAZINE

HELLO AND WELCOME!

I'm Indie Annie, and I'm thrilled you're reading this gorgeous full-color version of IAM. Did you know that you can also access all the information, education, and inspiration in our app? It's available on both the iOS App Store and Google Play. And for those that prefer to listen to me read articles, you can pop over to Spotify or our website. Happy Reading!

X

IndieAuthorMagazine.com

Download on the
App Store

GET IT ON
Google Play

Spotify

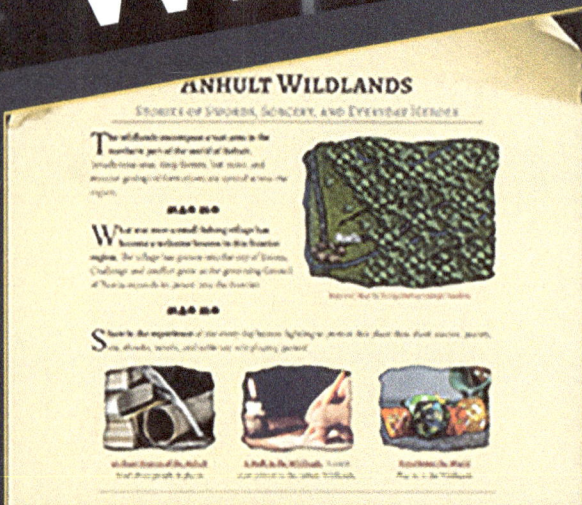

EMAIL MARKETING

ON THE COVER

REGULAR COLUMNS

THE WRITE LIFE

TYPEWRITER TALES

INDIE
AUTHOR MAGAZINE

EDITORIAL

Publisher | Chelle Honiker

Editor in Chief | Nicole Schroeder

Creative Director | Alice Briggs

Copy Editor | Lisa Thompson

ADVERTISING & MARKETING

Inquiries | Chelle Honiker
publisher@IndieAuthorMagazine.com

Information
https://IndieAuthorMagazine.com/
advertising/

CONTRIBUTORS

Angela Archer, Elaine Bateman, Patricia Carr, Bradley Charbonneau, Maria Connor, Honorée Corder, Jackie Dana, Jamie Davis, Laurel Decher, Fatima Fayez, Gill Fernley, Greg Fishbone, Eirynne Gallagher, Jac Harmon, Marion Hermannsen, Chrishaun Keller-Hanna, Michael La Ronn, Kasia Lasinska, Monica Leonelle, Megan Linski-Fox, Craig Martelle, Angie Martin, Kevin McLaughlin, Lasairiona McMaster, Jenn Mitchell, Susan Odev, Clare Sager, Grace Snoke, Joe Solari, Wendy Van Camp

SUBSCRIPTIONS
https://indieauthormagazine.com/subscribe/

HOW TO READ
https://indieauthormagazine.com/how-to-read/

WHEN WRITING MEANS BUSINESS
IndieAuthorMagazine.com

Athenia Creative | 6820 Apus Dr., Sparks, NV, 89436 USA | 775.298.1925
ISSN 2768-7880 (online)–ISSN 2768-7872 (print)

Design like a Pro for free

FROM THE PUBLISHER

THE POWER OF PERSONALITY

Back in the olden days of indie publishing, when the earth's crust was cooling and it was a wild west of new information for self-publishers, I was fortunate enough to attend a conference in Austin, Texas, with this month's featured subject, Tammi Labrecque.

It's hard to remember back that far. So much has changed since 2017.

But she's unforgettable, and I liked her immediately. She has strong opinions, and she's able to perfectly articulate them. She speaks with authority, yet she's utterly relatable, and she has the right answers for complicated questions about how to connect with readers in a format that baffles many authors.

When we were launching this magazine, she's who I turned to when we were writing our email onboarding sequences. I sent the drafts over to her, expecting some semblance of an "attagirl"—I was a copywriter and marketer, after all. I was looking for validation.

With her usual pull-no-punches style, she wrote back: "Dear Lord, Chelle. They make me want to set fire to my computer."

I died a little that day. But she was right.

And then she said, "You have all this amazing talent and personality wrapped up in your writers—use it. Write the emails from the perspective of Indie Annie."

Which, of course, was a genius idea, as Annie is an amalgam of our team and philosophy and corporate persona.

There's a lot of talk lately about artificial intelligence and how it will impact our industry. We're planning an entire issue to cover it, in fact. But there's one thing that I'm confident can't be replaced when it comes to connecting with your readers, and that's the power of your personality coming through. I'm sure you'll understand what I mean when you read Tammi's contribution as a writer to this month's issue, as well as our feature about her.

I hope you enjoy them and learn as much from her as I have.

To your success,
Chelle Honiker
Publisher
Indie Author Magazine

FROM THE EDITOR IN CHIEF

HOW DID YOU MEET YOUR WRITING GROUP?

One of this month's features asks a handful of authors that exact question, and I always love hearing people's responses. I met mine through Camp NaNoWriMo about eight years ago. (In fact, you can read about our group, the Treehouse of Writers, in the article!) During the summer sessions of the writing challenge, the site used to sort participants into "cabins," virtual chat rooms where you could cheer on one another. Most of our group found themselves in the same cabin from the start; I was lucky enough to stumble across them a few days later in the forums when my original cabin was a bit of a dud. They adopted me, and that was that.

We chatted incessantly that summer, keeping our cabin open for as long as we could. And when the website inevitably refreshed and locked us out, we migrated to other platforms to stay in touch. Since that first summer, we've continued to sprint with one another, encourage one another, and share our writing wins and woes. Beyond that, we've also become inseparable friends. And we still call each other nicknames based on our NaNoWriMo usernames, for old time's sake.

We live in multiple time zones and write in a variety of genres; if it weren't for that cabin chat room in 2015, I doubt any of us would've ever met in real life. But maybe your group's origin story is just as happenstance: an impromptu meeting at a writing conference, a decision to visit a new coffee shop one weekend instead of your usual hangout. As the four writers highlighted in this issue can attest, finding your people isn't really something you can plan, but it's undeniably magical when it happens. I know I'm forever grateful for the friendship I've found among the Treehouse and for the encouragement and glitter-infused joy they've brought to my writing and to my life. Here's wishing you all a chance to experience that magic for yourselves—and for those who already have, a chance to celebrate it this month with the ones who helped conjure it in the first place.

Nicole Schroeder
Editor in Chief
Indie Author Magazine

The Reader Experience

The reader experience is both subjective and objective. You can measure it in your reader recidivism: What's your read-through rate to the next title? Are you getting good numbers of reviews, more than each previous release? Is your book ranking better than it should based on sales?

Those are all signs of a positive reader experience. Did you get a bonus? That's also a sign of a positive reader experience since "reader delight" is now part of the criteria, though no one is really sure what goes into a bonus nowadays as it's far more than the straight number of page reads on the title.

Are your readers highlighting passages within the e-book? More signs of a positive reader experience.

It starts with writing the best book you can possibly write and then asking your readers to enjoy it, immerse themselves within it, and interact with the story. It's more than just borrowing the book in Kindle Unlimited and reading it. It's more than just buying it.

It's about readers embracing the story. This adds more importance to writing with the reader in mind. We're artists, and we create.

But we're also business moguls. There's no reason not to create, but we need to do so with an eye toward the recipient as opposed to just writing something on a whim and a stream of consciousness without ever taking into account how the recipient would experience the story. The former is how you can make money in this business.

You're not compromising any of your artistic creativity by thinking about the reader when you write. Isn't an artist's task to manipulate the perceptions of those who view the art? To create an experience they will not forget?

You don't have to write the best book ever written to create an incredible reader experience. It only has to keep them engaged and turning the pages. It's not as tall an order as it may seem. It was engaging in your mind. It can be engaging on paper. And then you can do it again because the more you practice, the better you get.

Create an unforgettable reader experience, and you will build the foundation of an incredible career. ◼

Craig Martelle

Dear Indie Annie,

I've started a new social media account to market my book, and I love posting photos and videos of the other things I read! But I get nervous posting anything about my own writing. How do I build up the confidence to market my work to strangers?

(Sort of) Social in Seville

DEAR SENSATIONAL SOCIAL,

What are you afraid of, my little social media butterfly? I guess you have followers, right? Avid readers who are looking to you for tips and suggestions about what to read next? They obviously agree with your choices. They like what you recommend. They like you. Chances are high that they will also like what you write.

But how can you be sure, my fluttery friend? Ah, there's the rub. You can't.

There are steps you can take, though, to test the waters and put your mind at rest. Ask your followers to beta read your stories.

I would begin by hinting in your posts that you have been working on something in your spare time. Share books, movies, or real events that have inspired your story. Check your comments section for people's reactions. Are you getting a lot of likes or interactions from a couple of really engaged individuals? They could be the foundation of your beta team. You could then put out a call on your social media to recruit readers and/or direct message those whom you have identified as the most supportive.

It would flatter most people who love the same books as you to be asked to help launch another author's career. Who doesn't want to be there on the ground floor? If you turn out to write a bestseller, they can boast they knew you when no one else did. They can share in your success.

Need help from your favorite Indie Aunt?
Ask Dear Indie Annie a question at
IndieAnnie@indieauthormagazine.com

You see, many have the distant dream of becoming a writer themselves, and you can invite them into your process.

In return, you'll get hopefully honest feedback on your stories before you release them into the big bad world. Remember, you are not asking them to edit your work. That is what your alpha team, including professional editors, would do. They may and probably will spot some typos, but most importantly they will help you get valuable feedback on the success of your story. In other words, they will let you know if they enjoy it.

And if they enjoy it, you'll no longer have followers—you'll have fans! Fans who will become your street team, pushing your books through their social media and leaving you positive reviews when the books are finally released.

"Oh, but Indie Annie," I hear you cry, "what if they don't like them?" That is a risk, I grant you, sweet Social. That is why you need to find several beta readers. One person's opinion is not fact. In fact, several people's opinions are not fact. However, if they all tell you that your story could be improved by changing the opening chapter or tightening up a soggy middle,

then perhaps that is something you can work on before publication.

I appreciate this idea is terrifying, but every successfully published author has been where you are now. No book will ever be perfect. No book will ever be universally applauded. Perhaps you will need to rewrite huge sections of your story before it is ready, but that, my dear, is part of the process.

I will take this opportunity to remind you about the books you have loved and posted about. Not everyone will have agreed with your selection, but you thought them worthy of support. I can promise you that if you reached out to those authors, they too could tell you about receiving painful critiques. They could also tell you that the biggest fear is fear itself.

So, as you have already dangled your feet in the social media pond, cast the line, and reel in your new fans. It will be an exciting adventure!

Happy writing,
Indie Annie

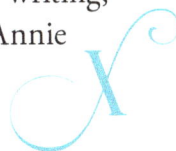

10 TIPS FOR
TWITTER

Twitter is a unique social media platform built on brevity, requiring users to limit posts to only 280 characters at a time. But a writer can pack plenty into these tiny tweets. For many authors, Twitter has become the cornerstone of their author platform, their way of getting the word out for a book launch or to promote a new journal publication.

Although it is not always the best place to develop readers, Twitter can be an excellent source for networking with fellow authors, editors, and small presses. And even with the advent of the platform's new management in late October 2022, engagement in the Twitter writing community is still strong. For many authors, Twitter is still a viable asset to their platform. These ten tips should guide you if you decide the site is right for you.

1 CREATE AN EASY-TO-READ PROFILE

A profile needs to tell a potential reader who you are at a glance. Make sure you have a clean headshot in your profile. Otherwise you'll come across as an "egg"—the default profile image for new users on the platform—and people might mistake you for a bot or a scammer.

Twitter bios can only be 160 characters, so space is at a premium. A good author tagline combined with hashtags describing your work is an effective way to approach the space. Also consider using hashtags for any writing organizations you belong to.

A banner for your Twitter account needs to be 1,600 × 500 pixels. Use this to showcase your book covers and connect the visual branding of your website to your Twitter account.

2 PIN A TWEET TO THE TOP OF YOUR TIMELINE

One of the first tasks you should do when starting a Twitter account is to create a pinned tweet at the top of your feed. If you did not put your tagline in your bio, this would be a good alternate spot for it. You might also use this as a space to list your social media links to allow interested people to find you on the internet. Some authors put links to their latest book here.

If you like a user's feed, it is a common practice on Twitter to retweet their pinned tweet. Make sure you tap into this convention.

3 USE AUTOMATION TO MANAGE YOUR PROMOTIONAL TWEETS

As an author, you want to keep your promotions consistent. Instead of retyping everything and being present to tweet them day and night, use an automated system to post the tweets for you. Create listings of your promotional tweets in a text document or in a spreadsheet. Make them easy to cut and paste directly to Twitter or into the automated server of your choice. These tweets should support your published articles, stories, poetry, and novels. Post regularly, at least a few times each day. However, never allow the automated promotions to be over 25 percent of your total tweeting. Pick a time each day to manually retweet topics of interest to your readers.

Pro Tip: Set up a social media scheduler to post promotional tweets to your account at regular intervals. I use SocialOomph (https://socialoomph.com) to manage my Twitter account. It is a paid service. Users can create "buckets" of dozens of pre-written tweets that rotate into their feed on a regular basis. They can also create limited-time promotions on the fly. Other options include Buffer or Hootsuite. Both have a limited-use free service to allow you to test the program and see if it is right for you. For me, it has been worth the cost to save time and know my promotions are going out every day, even if I'm sick or on vacation.

4 CREATE PRIVATE LISTS

Twitter has a feature that allows you to create lists of users, which you can set to be private or public. Each list allows you to follow that user in a special feed. Use the lists to monitor what is going on with people who interest you or could be useful in your writing career. If you belong to writing organizations, set up a private list of all the members of the group on Twitter. Each group can have its own list. If you want to meet editors or agents, set up a private list of ones you meet on Twitter, and use the list to monitor their public comments and get to know them. This can become a powerful communication tool and cut through the noise on Twitter.

Pro Tip: Subscribe to public lists of other writers. Often, they will have extensive lists of their own, and it is easy to use these public lists in your retweeting plan. Just remember that you do not own these lists. If the other user leaves Twitter, they may take their list with them.

5 RETWEET OTHERS

In marketing, there is the 80/20 rule, also known as the Pareto Principle: Spend 80 percent of the time promoting others, and use the other 20 percent of the time to promote yourself. Set aside ten to fifteen minutes once or twice a day to go through your lists on Twitter and find topics to retweet. Most of the time, a simple retweet is enough. Comments on the retweets help to drive more engagement, but they can take a great deal of time. Only comment if you feel you are adding to the conversation.

Pro Tip: As a writer and poet, I've found that focusing retweets on open calls to magazines, podcast programs about writing, or famous magazines' articles can be popular choices. My fellow wordsmiths are always looking for fresh places to publish, and it costs me nothing but a few seconds to point out sources or articles of interest.

6 DEVELOP LISTS OF USEFUL HASHTAGS

Twitter uses hashtags in users' tweets as searchable terms on the platform, cutting across the noise and giving your tweets tremendous reach with people who are not following you. Most communities have their own hashtags, and learning what these are is vital to you as an author. Hashtags such as #BookTwt, #WritingCommunity, or #PoetryCommunity are great places to start, but search the internet or look at tweets by other authors to find more specific hashtags for your writing as well. Group any hashtags you gather in a text file—this makes using them in your posts as easy as a simple cut and paste.

7 LIKE YOUR MENTIONS AND RETWEETS

Twitter is such a vast sea of people, it is easy to get lost in the shuffle. Therefore, whenever you receive a notification that someone has mentioned you or retweeted one of your posts on their own feed, be sure to like it. When another person sees you took the time to respond to them, it helps to create a better bond and makes you more memorable. It's also considered good Twitter etiquette.

8 ALL TWEETS ARE FOREVER

Always remember that while Twitter is easy to use and seems fleeting, it is a permanent record. What you say in a tweet can come back years later and harm you. Never tweet in anger. Use your words responsibly.

9 USE IMAGES TO CONVEY MORE INFORMATION

Use graphic software to create images to go with your tweets. Images can create emotions, showcase poetry or book excerpts, and show off your latest cover. Images draw the eye and can give your tweet more impact in your reader's feed.

Pro Tip: Use a graphic design program like Canva to create branded images for your author platform. Create images to support published poems or short stories. You can highlight an award nomination or showcase a book launch. Don't feel the need to reinvent the wheel; it's easy to repurpose your images for all parts of your platform, be it website, Facebook, or Twitter.

10 ENGAGE IN COMMUNITIES

There are many writing communities on Twitter: pitch days to agents, writers sharing tips, editors looking for submissions, podcasters asking for guests. It pays to read your tweet lists for relevant information and interact with others to cement connections. Twitter can be a wonderful tool for finding new writing jobs, promoting projects, and keeping up with what is going on in the writing industry. Its character limits and short-form content might make it a rare bird among other sites, but find the tricks to make it work for you, and it can become a powerful addition in your social media roster. ■

Wendy Van Camp

Newsletter Ninja

TAMMI LABRECQUE SHARES LESSONS ON BALANCE, IMPOSTOR SYNDROME, AND MAKING EMAIL MARKETING LOOK EASY

Even if you've never met her before, one conversation with Tammi Labrecque is probably enough for the two of you to become friends.

The author and course creator is bright, bubbly, and—even on a Friday afternoon—ready to talk your ear off about all things publishing. She's spent almost a decade in the indie sphere writing in a variety of genres. "I kind of dabble in everything," she says. But these days, she's probably best recognized as the "newsletter ninja." Her two-book nonfiction series of the same name has offered nearly twenty thousand authors tips for perfecting their mailing list and attracting new readers, an often underappreciated resource Tammi says can make a big difference for keeping fans invested in your work. But she didn't realize she had a knack for it until years into her career.

"People would be just talking about their newsletters … and I'd say, 'Oh, why don't you try X?' Or 'I was thinking about doing Y, you know, if I ever finish this book,'" she says. "And what happened over and over again was people would say, 'Oh my God, where did you hear that?' And I would say, 'I made it up in my head. It just seemed like a good idea.'"

Tammi's career as an indie author began in 2014, but her work as an author arguably began even earlier,

with a traditional publishing contract she received to be part of an anthology. As someone who grew up loving to write, the acceptance was a boost in her confidence in her own talent for storytelling—even more so when she realized how difficult that market typically was. Still, aside from that short story she submitted, she wasn't able to publish the work she queried for several years following. And it wasn't until she was fired from her office job that she began to consider alternate avenues to publication.

As a reader and writer, she'd followed the rise of independent publishing for a few years. So when she faced the prospect of finding another traditional nine-to-five, Tammi instead turned the ordeal into an opportunity to launch her book business.

"I did really well in that first year that I was publishing," she says. In a still-emerging market, it was easier for readers to find her books. But though she was managing to make a full-time living from her fiction at the start, there was one pitfall, she admits: "I write slow." She took up editing to continue to support her and her kids, until editing projects started to take over her writing time entirely. Finally, conversations she was having with other authors convinced her to shift her focus to newsletters. She published *Newsletter Ninja: How to Become an Author Mailing List Expert*, in the summer of 2018, and the second in the series released early last year.

WHAT A READER WANTS

What makes newsletters so intuitive for her? Tammi says it's her ability to see things from a reader's point of view. "Because I'm a little bit compulsive and I have ADHD, which can result in a hyperfocus sort of thing, I am a superfan of things," she says. "I don't feel lukewarm about anything ever. … When people are like, what might my subscribers like? I'm like, 'Oh, I'll tell

you what subscribers would like because if I was your superfan, this is what I would want.'"

Even so, she says, a lot of her suggestions are only her opinion and will depend on several factors. "There's so many variables at any given time that I can almost never give anybody stock advice." She's almost adopted the phrase "it depends" as a mantra; the medium necessitates it.

The several courses and workshops Tammi has offered over the years have included plenty of individualized input and direction from Tammi herself, based on everything from someone's genre to the size of their mailing list. She admits it's often taken away from the time she can devote to her own fiction. "For a long time, I really struggled with that, with being the person who was helping other authors instead of being a bestseller myself," she says. Yet she doesn't hesitate to say her work as a "ninja" is also her proudest accomplishment.

In recent years, the world of independent publishing has become more crowded than when Tammi started publishing, and visibility has become all the more important for authors to prioritize. The one piece of advice Tammi offers that can be widely applicable is to recognize you aren't bothering your readers by emailing them.

"They signed up to hear from you! You could not have a more explicit indication that they want to hear from you than the fact that they gave you their email address," she says with a laugh. She encourages authors to talk with their readers regularly about the things going on in their lives, even if the topic isn't always book related.

SECRETS TO SUCCESS

Even with her years of focus on newsletters and the support and testimonials she's received from other authors in the past—well-known names like authors David Gaughran, Chris Fox, and Rachel McLean—Tammi admits she still deals with impostor syndrome when talking about newsletters, as well as with her own writing. Although outside validation helps, she says she also believes in a "fake it until you make it" mentality and takes comfort in recognizing what she still has left to learn.

She's also dealt with burnout in the past, which she says comes with an easier solution, if harder to put into practice. After she hit burnout working on creating the second Newsletter Ninja book, initially about newsletter automations, she was forced to cancel the preorder and took time in 2020 to reset her focus and let herself recover. As the months passed, she realized she didn't feel like she was in a place to speak about the more technical side of email marketing yet—but she did have advice to give regarding reader magnets. *Newsletter Ninja 2: If*

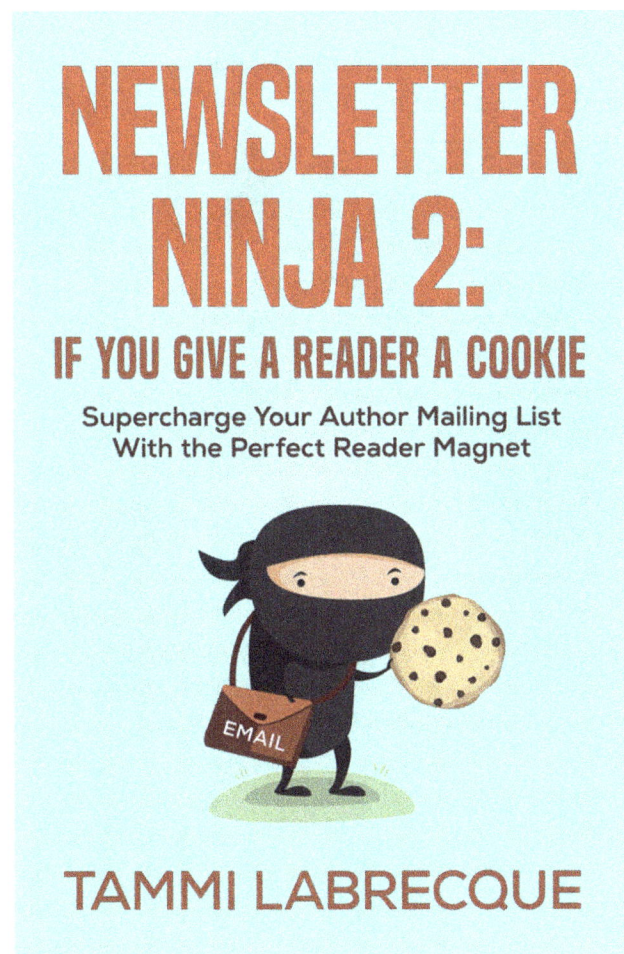

You Give a Reader a Cookie is a shorter book than the first in the series—"which, believe me, I heard about in reviews," Tammi says, "but I'm also not one to pad." The book, like the first, boasts thousands of readers who've learned from her advice.

In writing it, Tammi came to learn an important skill, too, about balancing her work on newsletters with her own writing. "I sort of stepped back and I took stock, and I was like … the reason this never gets to the place it needs to be is because I'm always splitting my focus," she says. Soon after the release of the second Newsletter Ninja book, Tammi paused her own writing goals and focused solely on her email marketing business, with a goal to put words on paper again at the beginning of this year.

It's a lesson we can all learn from in a way, Tammi says: Your book business doesn't have to look a certain way in order for you to consider yourself an author. "People can still make it in this business," she says. "I see them do it every day. … But you need to evaluate what your definition of being successful is so that you can temper your expectations."

She continues, "I didn't write for however many months, April through the end of the year, and I'm still a writer. I know people who are only making a few hundred dollars a month and they are not six-figure authors; it is true. But they are writers, and they have a handful of readers who really love them. And next year, they'll have another handful."

Tammi's readers are out there too, even if they don't realize it yet. The Monday after our interview, she finally returned to the fiction draft that's been waiting in the wings for her, the one she's most excited about seeing completed. It's still a work in progress for now, she says, but it's the project she's closest to finishing. And you can bet when she does, her superfans will be there to help her celebrate. ◼

Nicole Schroeder

The Secret Mindset of a Millionaire Author

Millionaire authors can seem so grandiose. It's hard to imagine an author making six figures a year from their work, let alone ten times that amount. Despite the apparent monstrosity of this task, there are many indie authors achieving this monument every year. Perhaps they know something the general public doesn't—or perhaps they think differently than most authors do. Are seven-figure authors really that different from the everyday writer, and is there advice these publishing dynamos can give to help elevate the dreams of others?

Lee Savino is a seven-figure author with a collection of over two hundred English and translated titles in the Paranormal, Urban Fantasy, and Sci-Fi genres. Savino went the traditional route of going to college and landing a conventional career but discovered she wasn't happy. Her heart was in writing books, and one day, she decided to take the leap and become a full-time author. After years of publishing, she managed to accumulate her publishing expertise into a seven-figure author career.

"The biggest common denominator was we [my coauthor and I] wanted to make money from our books and we were okay with making money from our books. When I started out, I wanted to make money, but I wasn't allowing myself to make money," Savino says. "It can be helpful to dig into any resistance you have."

For many years after publishing her first novel, Savino struggled to increase her author income. She'd plateaued around thirty thousand dollars and wasn't able to increase her income beyond that rate until she looked into changing her mindset.

"I used to believe you have to work hard and do something you hate in order to get paid well. I also used to believe rich people are all bad and evil, and I didn't want to be evil, so I made sure I didn't make above a certain amount," Savino says. She had to change that mindset in order to become a bestseller, and that meant allowing her subconscious to lead the way rather than her conscious mind.

"When you let go, you're able to create, and creation comes from the subconscious mind creating, versus the conscious mind, which is the manager mind," Savino says. "And if you're critical of yourself, you're shutting yourself down."

One of the most optimal ways Savino helps to control her ego is to practice exercises in letting go of fear. "I talk about goal setting and putting stuff out there and writing it down, but it can be helpful to write something down and put it in a box, then let it go," Savino says. "What happens is your subconscious mind works on solving the problem."

Savino says her routine varies, and that she doesn't put pressure on herself, which is key to generating success.

"I dither around for an hour with social media and emails, and try to do a good chunk of writing in the morning, then I'll go to yoga, because I used to sit in bed and write all day, and now I have back issues," Savino says. "Taking care of your health and paying attention to pain is becoming increasingly important. After yoga, I goof off—I could write again, but I usually book a lot of meetings."

Savino's schedule remains untethered, and she insists that every day is different, with her responsibilities requiring her to wear a lot of hats. "I have a busy business with all these things to do," she says. "There's a lot of moving parts, so there's more to my business now than writing one book a year in English."

One of her most

powerful tips for achieving seven figures for authors is to learn to delegate the tasks that you don't have to do, while focusing on the tasks that you're best at. "It's okay to be yourself. I had a goal of being a millionaire author, but that doesn't have to be anyone's goal, and you don't have to be alone," Savino says. "Hire people to help you, because that's what it's about. You want to write the book, but once it's done, you get help. Do the things that only you can do, and the things that you can do, but someone else can do too, hire that out. Use brain power, and delegate things to get off your plate." Though this might sound like an impossible summit for a new indie author, Savino encourages that finding help doesn't have to break the bank, as she often traded services with other authors early in her career to find the assistance she needed.

"Start where you are. Hire who you can; barter with other authors, do beta read and editing swaps, because you can learn a lot from critiquing someone else. You need to find out what in your business is necessary," Savino says. "Then, if you're grouchy about your progress, look at where you are, look at where you want to be, and then look back at where you started. That's gratitude, which is super helpful for your mindset."

Savino also suggests that authors do a lot of experimenting to find their niche in different markets. "Look at the top-selling series. Ask yourself how you can do it better, or if you decide to write something different, hop

around and experiment," Savino says. "For me, it was about taking the money coming in and investing it in ads, BookBubs, newsletters. Try to find more readers and build your mailing list, because you want to have fans you can touch over and over again. Put some of that investment into audiobooks, then do translations. Ideally, all these moving parts enable you to do something even better, then bring all your fans with you while finding new ones."

She encourages authors to keep pushing forward, especially if they see potential in a new series.

"If you can make fifty thousand [dollars] a year, you can make a hundred thousand. If you can make a hundred thousand, you can definitely make seven figures," Savino says. "You've gotten readers who like your stuff, so now it's about getting more readers, and there are always more readers. Your fellow authors are never your competition, because they are always helping you bring more people into the market, and if you're jealous of another author, it's because you believe you can't have what they have.

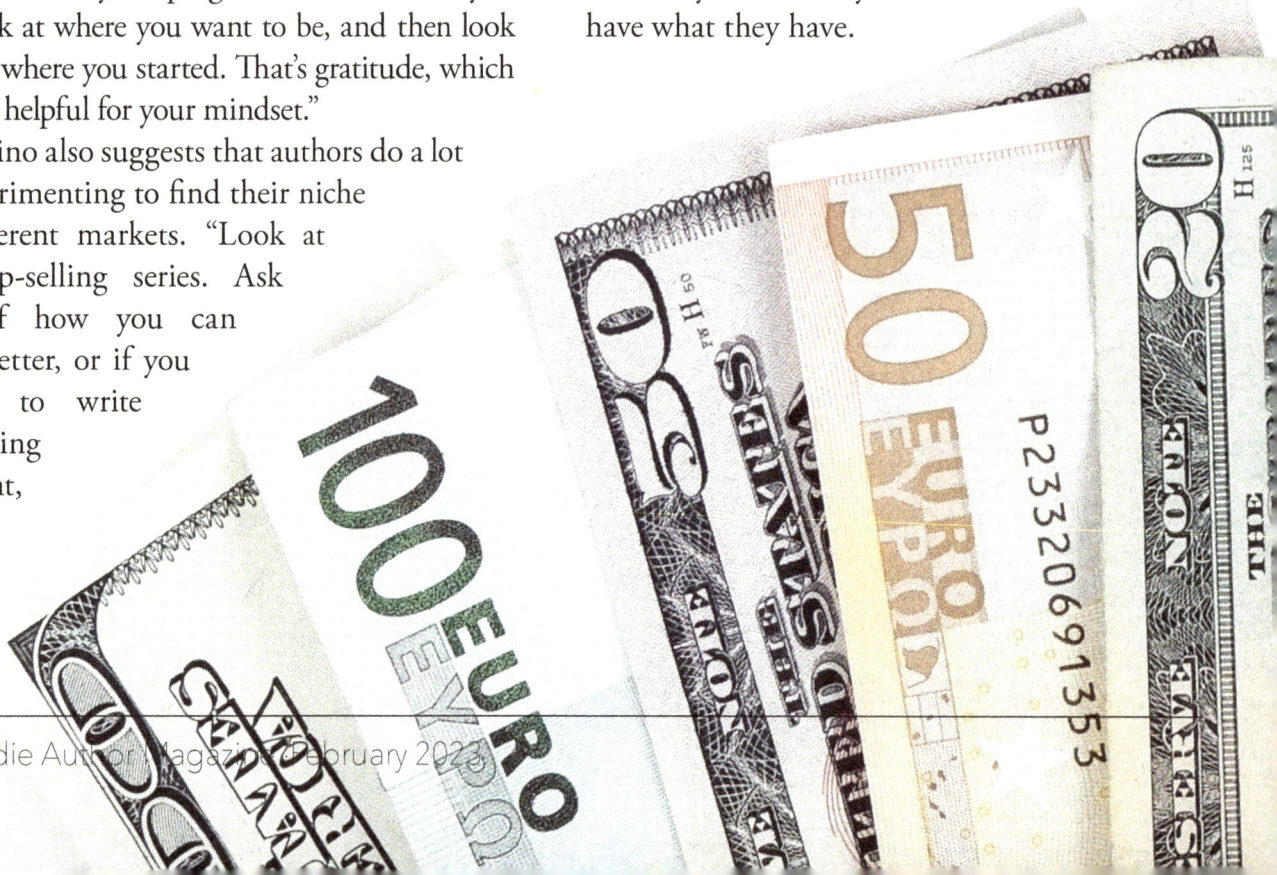

"Colleen Hoover is finding new readers every single week. This market is infinite, and you will never reach all your readers. It's just a matter of scaling," Savino continues. "Ask yourself how to take your intellectual property and sell it in different formats and languages. Reinvest your money so you can have more reach."

Of course, experimenting with platforms and different avenues of media entertainment takes financial risk, but Savino knows that the more an author is willing to take risks, the greater potential of returns for their career.

"The most successful authors know if they lose money, they'll get it back," Savino says. They know they're not a bad person or unworthy because they lost money, and they're not afraid to make money and lose it all again. It's all because they know they're good enough as they are."

Savino believes that within a few years, indie authors will be producing graphic novels, webtoons, animation, theme music, and even films for their own work. "First comes the intention that you want something that big. It some-

times doesn't feel that safe to be that rich, but we're on this planet to have fun and do what we want, so you have to ask yourself what you want. Because if it pops in your head and you want it, you're meant to have it."

Above all, Savino insists, there's one key to having a seven-figure author career, and that's self-love, accepting yourself as you are wherever you might be in your business and not pressuring yourself to be more than what you're able to be at the current moment.

"It becomes an exercise in raising your own self-esteem, unconditionally loving yourself—not when you finish the book or when you hit [the] *New York Times*, but right now, and knowing you don't have to prove yourself. I thought by reaching these goals everyone would celebrate me and I'd be good enough, but I can celebrate myself and be good enough right now, even if I'm getting out of bed at noon."

Lee Savino is an author of Paranormal, Sci-Fi, Dark, and Contemporary Romance that leaves a lasting impression. She also teaches courses on millionaire author mindset, which can be found at https://millionaire-author-coaching.teachable.com/courses. You can discover her books at https://leesavino.com. ■

Megan Linski-Fox

The Art of Story-Selling

HOW TO STRUCTURE YOUR EMAILS AND USE YOUR STORYTELLING POWERS TO SELL MORE BOOKS

Our brains are wired for stories. And as an author, you are a natural storyteller, with the ability to craft compelling narratives and engage readers in a way that few others can. So why not use those same storytelling skills to help sell your books? By leveraging the power of email marketing, you can reach out to potential readers and use your storytelling prowess not just to write your books but to get more book sales as well.

Stories have connected us for thousands of years, so it makes sense to use stories to build a relationship with your audience. But before we delve into the specifics of how to do this, we need to understand the importance of "giving value" in email marketing. "Giving value" is something that many people associate with giving stuff away for free, whether that's free content, free expertise, or free hard teaching. Precisely because it's free, people often perceive that information as having a lower value.

But these days, giving value means offering something of worth to your readers in exchange for their attention. There's no such thing as a free lunch, and if you want to nurture a relationship with your list, you've got to work at it. The key is to give your readers a reason to pay attention to your emails and take action, rather than simply sending them a hard sell for your book.

Value can be as simple as making someone feel something, whether that's with an uplifting moment, an entertaining anecdote that gives them a chuckle, or a new way of thinking about something. You can talk about your books, the inspiration for your characters, or even give a behind-the-scenes glimpse into your life.

You know how the endings of some books and movies leave the audience feeling cheated, whereas some give you that warm hug feeling? Ideally, you want your readers to feel closer to the latter—they should believe that the time they spend reading your emails is well spent, so they'll be more inclined to open the next one.

So what should you write about in your emails to give value to your readers and entice them to buy your book? Here are a few ideas:

- **Behind-the-scenes glimpses:** Give your readers a sneak peek at your writing process, including the inspiration behind your book, any challenges you faced while writing it, and how you overcame those challenges. This helps to build a connection with your readers and makes them feel like they are getting an inside look at your work.
- **Exclusive content:** Offer your readers exclusive content they can't get anywhere else, such as bonus chapters, character bios, or deleted scenes. This helps to create a sense of exclusivity and makes your readers feel special.
- **Personal stories:** Share personal stories or experiences that relate to your book or its themes. This helps to humanize you as an author and gives your readers a deeper understanding of your work.
- **Tips and resources:** Provide your readers with valuable tips or resources related to your book's topic or genre. This helps to establish you as an expert in your field and gives your readers a reason to continue following your emails.

A SIMPLE EMAIL STRUCTURE

It's no good writing a great email if it won't get opened. Until you establish a strong bond with your readers and the mere sight of your name in their inbox will get your email opened, writing a compelling subject line is crucial. It strongly influences whether they will open your email. It's always a good idea to include keywords related to your book or theme that are relevant to your readers, so try crafting a subject line that is both attention-grabbing and informative.

Now that you have an idea of what to write about, let's talk about how to structure your emails to get people to click the link and buy your book. There is no right or wrong way to do it, nor is there a golden rule for the things you should write about. As your email list grows, you'll get a feel for what your audience responds to and engages with. From there, you'll be able to develop a consistent style that feels natural to you and is recognizable for your readers.

A common way to structure your email is by using the HTOC formula. The "H" stands for hook, not to be mistaken for the hook on your book description. Here, the hook is the story that will keep your reader's attention. You can use your storytelling techniques throughout: Turn yourself into a character, make yourself real in your reader's minds, and use storytelling techniques, such as setting the scene, introducing characters, and building tension, to engage your readers and keep them interested in your email. Also try personalizing your emails by using your readers' names and referencing their previous interactions with you. This helps to build a sense of connection and makes your emails more relevant to your readers.

"T" is for transition. This is where you connect your story to the main point of your email. It can be difficult to know how to transition from a story to a sales offer without coming across as too pushy, but that comes with practice. Try something as simple as asking a question—for example, "Have you ever experienced this? It's exactly what the main character in my new book faces." A good transition ties in neatly with your story and your offer.

That brings us to "O," for offer—the thing you're selling or promoting. Sometimes it helps to work backwards when planning your email. Think about the goal of your email and what you're selling. Are you promoting your backlist, a new release, or a social media post? Starting with the end goal in mind can help to give you direction. Equally, it can be fun just to write without knowing the end goal and seeing where it takes you.

And finally, end with "C," the call-to-action. Readers aren't mind readers; you need to tell them what you want them to do. Click a link, download, preorder, check out a book promotion—whatever it is, be clear and concise about what you want people to do. Include a link that works and that allows your subscribers to take the next step easily.

The HTOC formula showcases the opportunity we're already offering our readers: the chance to read a good story. It's also already used effectively by several authors. Just take Dean Koontz—the international bestselling author pens his author newsletters with the same four-part structure. Luckily you don't have to sign up for his emails, as he also posts them on his website, https://deankoontz.com/. You can read one he wrote a couple of years ago here: https://deankoontz.com/the-voice-of-the-night-now-available-with-new-audio/.

There are other ways to structure your emails, and you really don't need lots of fancy graphics. All you're aiming for is for your email to feel like a conversation between you and your reader. Your stories don't have to be epic; they don't even have to be yours. They could be about something you read in the news.

There really isn't a right or wrong way to structure your emails, and it's totally OK to evolve your email style as you grow. But by using these tips as a starting place, you can leverage your story-telling skills over time to create engaging and effective emails that will help you sell more books.

Now that you're armed with a simple formula, why not try it out in your next email? Remember to focus on giving value to your readers and use a clear call-to-action to encourage them to take the next step—just like the one you're reading now, as a matter of fact. With practice and time, you'll be well on your way to writing emails just as engaging and successful as the books they advertise. ■

Angela Archer

How to Roll out the Welcome Mat to Your Mailing List in Four Simple Steps

A quick glance in my crystal ball tells me you're reading this in February, but—because of the crazy scheduling required to produce a magazine like *Indie Author Magazine*—I'm actually writing these words in November, having just returned from 20Books Vegas.

While I was there, I spent some time chatting with Chelle Honiker, *IAM*'s illustrious publisher, about newsletter topics I might write about, and we kept coming back to welcome sequences.

Welcome sequences are one of the most popular topics I get asked about, and that might be why we kept circling back to it. (It might also have been the gin.) These introductory emails you write about yourself and your books can be essential to keeping people invested in what you have to tell them. Except the thing about welcome sequences is that they are so individual that they're hard to talk about except in the most general terms—because so much depends on your genre, your backlist, how often you publish, or where your subscribers come from.

GUEST AUTHOR TAMMI LABRECQUE

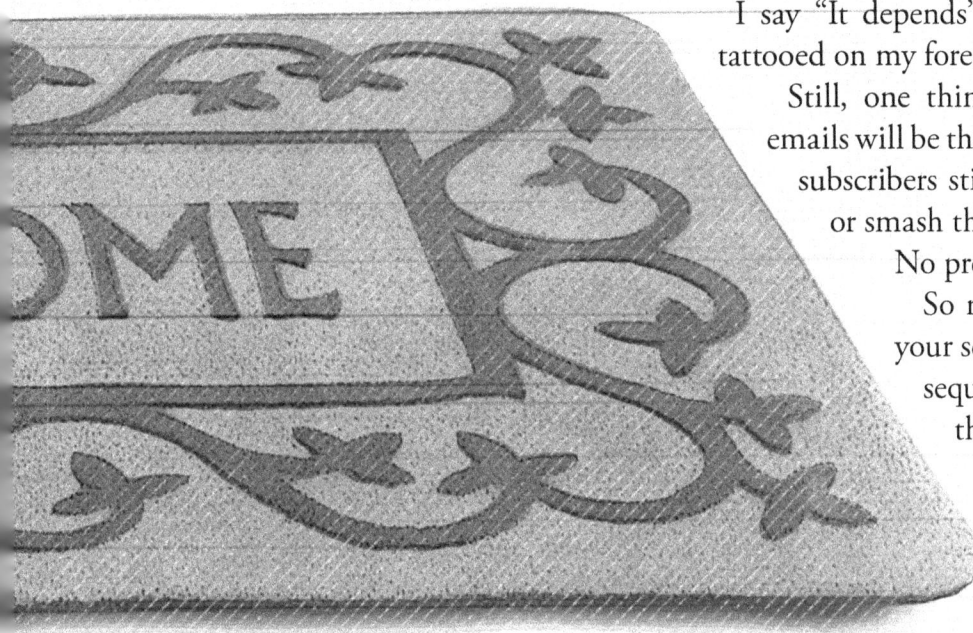

I say "It depends" so much, I should just get it tattooed on my forehead.

Still, one thing is universal: Those first few emails will be the deciding factor in whether your subscribers stick around to become superfans or smash the Unsubscribe link.

No pressure, right?

So rather than talk about how long your sequence should be, or how many sequences you should have, or any of the tech you have to master to get readers through them, let's talk instead about what to include in your first few emails, however many there are, in order to ensure that subscribers understand right from the start why they should care about you and what you write.

There are four key bits of info that writers should aim to include when introducing themselves to subscribers. Together, they comprise a sort of origin story or mission statement that's unique to you.

The four basic elements are

1. who you are,
2. what you write,
3. why you write it, and
4. how you write it differently than anyone else in your genre.

If you don't know those four things, you'll struggle to set yourself apart from the pack—and you definitely want to set yourself apart from the pack. You're trying to build superfans here, and you can't do that by being just like everyone else who writes books like yours.

1. WHO YOU ARE

What you choose to reveal here is up to your level of comfort.

You can be specific enough to be relatable without revealing too much:

- "I'm a midwestern stay-at-home mom with limited time and a towering TBR pile, but when I couldn't find the sort of books I wanted to read, I decided to take Maya Angelou's advice and write them … you know, in the twelve minutes per day that the kids are napping."
- "I'm a lifelong engineer and reluctant big-city dweller who finally retired to ten acres in the middle of nowhere and started writing the kind of Science Fiction I loved as a kid."
- "I'm a recent college graduate and giant Tolkien fan, living the dream and writing the Epic Fantasy novels I've been daydreaming about for years."

Or you can just let it all hang out:

- "I live in South Bend, Indiana, with one hubby, two rambunctious toddlers, and three cats. I've always loved Romance novels, but these days I don't see a lot of heroines like me—I haven't worn a pair of high heels in three years, and I've got spit-up on my shirt right now—so I decided I'd be the one to write them."
- "I spent twenty years as head of development at Boston Engineering, but now I'm starting Phase 2: a working farm in

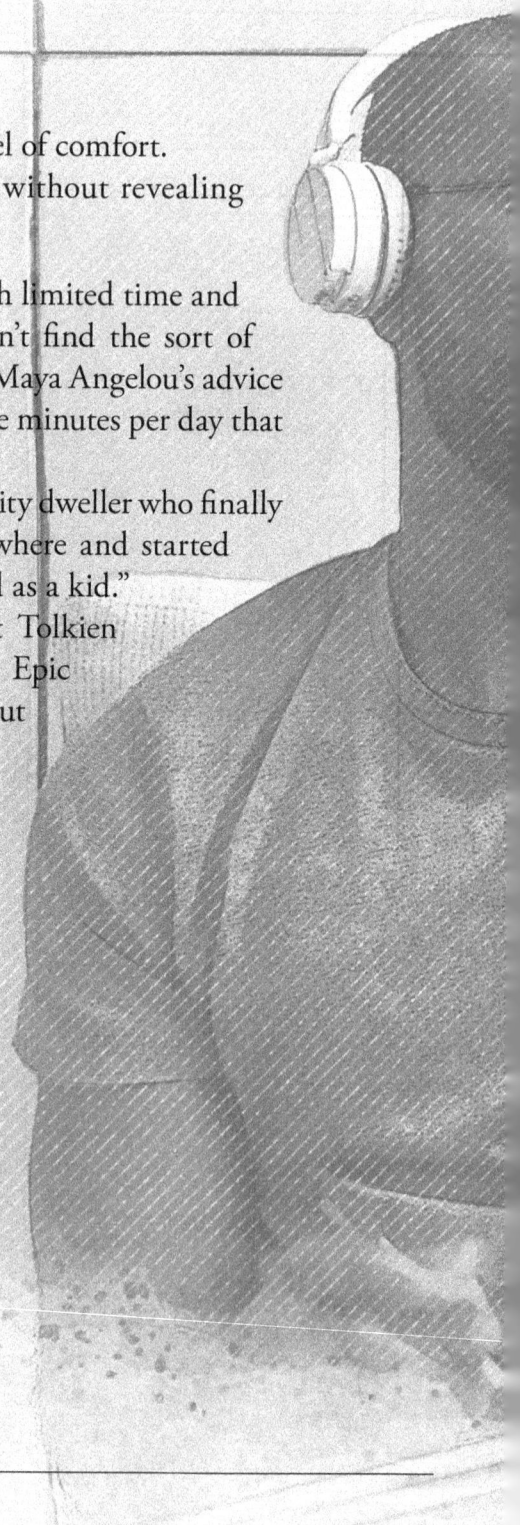

Western Massachusetts and a part-time career exploring deep space and the concept of the Singularity."

- "I'm fresh out of UC Santa Cruz with a boatload of student debt, but I decided that actually using my psychology degree wouldn't be as much fun as writing books about magic and dragons. My parents are thrilled!"

2. WHAT YOU WRITE

This can be straightforward—you're just letting readers know they're in the right place and they've found someone who writes the sort of books they like. If your genre covers a particularly wide range, be sure to elaborate on the types of stories your readers will find from you: "sword-and-sorcery Fantasy with dragons" or "super spicy small-town Romance," for example, instead of broad category names like "Fantasy" or "Romance."

3. WHY YOU WRITE IT

The usual answer to this is "Because I like it." But let's go a little deeper. (If you don't know why you write what you write, maybe this is the time to dig down and find out.)

- "I write Thrillers that keep you on the edge of your seat. I love the feeling of not being able to put a book down, and that's exactly what I want to do to my readers as well."
- "I write sword-and-sorcery Fantasy with dragons. I've loved Fantasy since I was a teenager, but it hasn't always reflected me or the people around me; I wanted to do my part to expand what was possible in the genre."
- "I write super-spicy small-town Romance. I love a Romance full of all the feels and steamy scenes galore, but I couldn't help wishing some of these women would grow a bit of a backbone."

4. HOW YOU WRITE IT DIFFERENTLY

Here, you want to tell readers what's special about your books as compared with someone else's. You hinted at this already with your "why," above. But now, when you lay out how you write something that fills that need, it will paint a picture for readers that will help them understand what they can reliably expect from your books—and potentially what matters to you most as a storyteller.

- "I write Thrillers that keep you on the edge of your seat. I love the feeling of not being able to put a book down, and that's exactly what I want to do to my readers as well, so I make sure readers don't know which of my characters you can trust to tell the truth."
- "I write women-led sword-and-sorcery Fantasy with dragons, but without the chain mail bikinis. I've loved Fantasy since I was a teenager, but it hasn't always reflected me or the

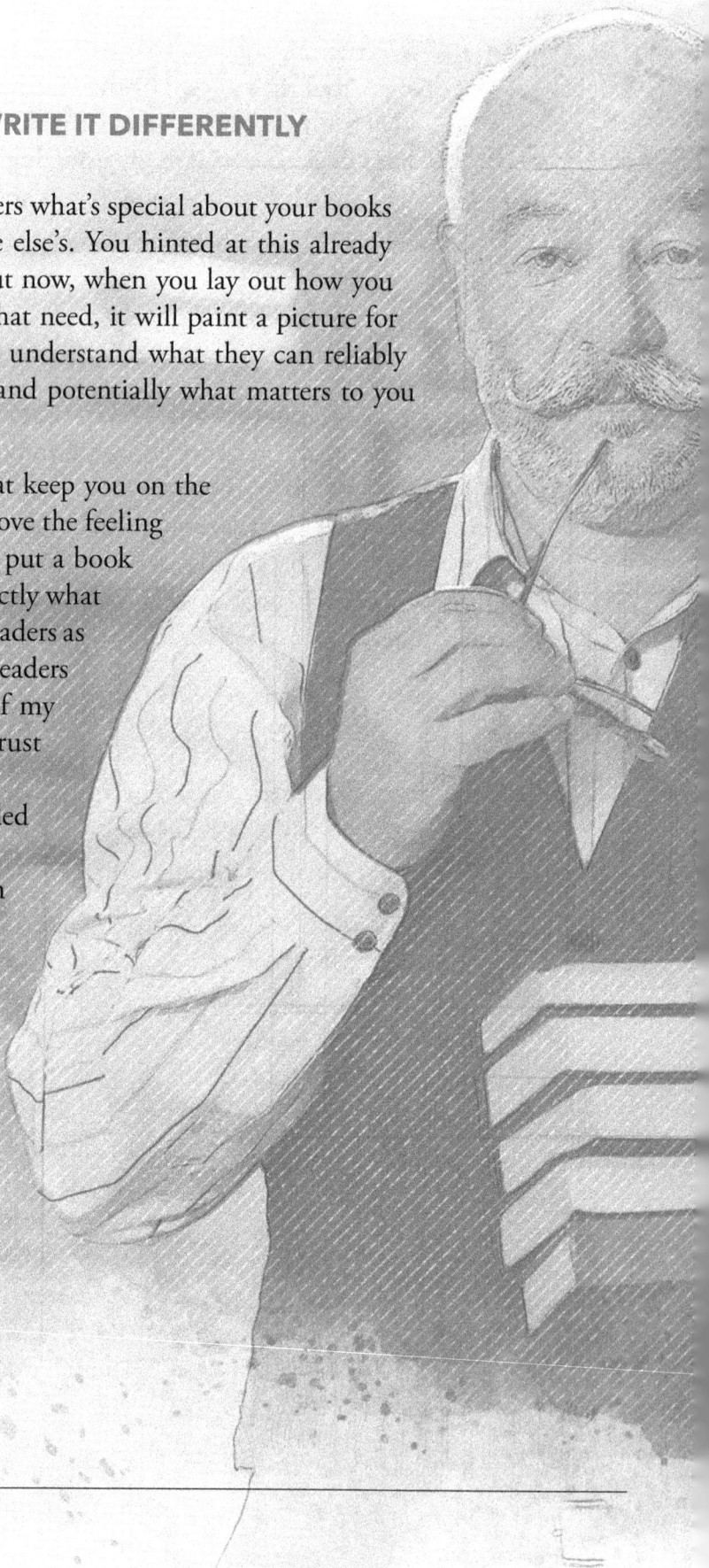

people around me; I wanted to do my part to expand what was possible in the genre."

• "I write super-spicy small-town Romance with heroines who know their worth—and heroes who actually deserve them. I love a Romance full of all the feels and steamy scenes galore, but I couldn't help wishing some of these women would grow a bit of a backbone."

Now that you know the steps to the perfect welcome sequence, I want you to get these answers down on paper and refine them so they're short, easy to remember, and repeatable. If you tell readers exactly what's so great about you, you give them the language to tell other people what's so great about you. You're making yourself recommendable. And you will hear them use this language to describe you to other readers, and you'll see it in reviews.

You can drop all four elements into one email—probably early in your welcome sequence for maximum benefit—or you can parse it out over a couple of emails; that's up to you.

As with so much else in your welcome sequence … all together now: "It depends." ■

Tammi Labrecque

A Bolt from the Sendinblue

SMS TEXTS AND UNLIMITED SUBSCRIBERS HELP SET THE EMAIL SERVICE PROVIDER APART

Amid the crowded marketplace of email providers, Sendinblue (https://sendinblue.com) is an often overlooked option. This French-based company has branch offices all over the globe and has services that easily rival some of its biggest competitors: Mailchimp, MailerLite, SendFox, and ActiveCampaign. But it's not simply a mail service—it's a comprehensive digital marketing platform.

Sendinblue offers email services that include automation, contact management, templates, and a drag-and-drop design feature, but it also goes further with extras like a landing page builder, SMS marketing, chatbot integration, e-commerce integration, and website tracking. Plus, the platform provides extensive analytics to help you track performance.

INTERACTION BEYOND THE INBOX

Sendinblue's integrated platform can make it easier to reach readers on other platforms. With the Conversations tool, authors can connect with people via SMS messages, web chat, and the unified hub for Facebook and Instagram pages and WhatsApp Business accounts. From here, users can deliver promotional offers, process orders, troubleshoot customer problems, and more—all in one centralized dashboard.

Moreover, Sendinblue's AI-driven technology can help automate conversations to improve engagement by responding faster and more accurately than a human would be able to. Thanks to automated greeting bots that can understand natural language processing (NLP), customers can interact with someone without feeling like they're talking to a robot and without requiring you to sacrifice writing time to manage the conversation.

Additionally, Sendinblue offers valuable tools for those running e-commerce businesses or taking payments online, such as fraud detection and advanced order management capabilities. It also integrates with many popular business apps, such as Google Ads, WordPress, or Facebook Ads, providing detailed analytics to track performance across channels.

SMS MARKETING: WHY IT MATTERS FOR AUTHORS

A study commissioned by Asurion and conducted by research firm Solidea Solutions in 2019 found that Americans, on average, check their phones ninety-six times per day. This suggests SMS, or text, marketing could be a more immediate way to connect with readers than other channels like email or social media. And because people are

Setup > Recipients > Confirmation

Your campaign is ready to be sent!

Review the report below before sending your campaign.

✅ **Setup**   142 Characters | **1 SMS**   Return to this step

From: 7752981975

Message: Indie Author Magazine
Read the January Issue Now: Visit https://indieauthormagazine.com/my-account/
Reply with STOP to opt-out of all messages

✅ **Recipients**   Total number of recipients: 0   Return to this step

Mailing lists: Test Mails

already becoming accustomed to receiving text messages from companies and brands, they're more likely to pay attention to them.

SMS messages are most effectively used for time-sensitive messages with a single call-to-action, such as reminding readers about upcoming book releases or promotions. They should be used sparingly—although they're great for immediacy, the practice can also backfire and annoy users if messages are sent too often, go on for too long, or include information better communicated in email. Consider SMS messages for sending readers exclusive content, such as a sneak peek of an upcoming book chapter. This offers readers an incentive to keep up with

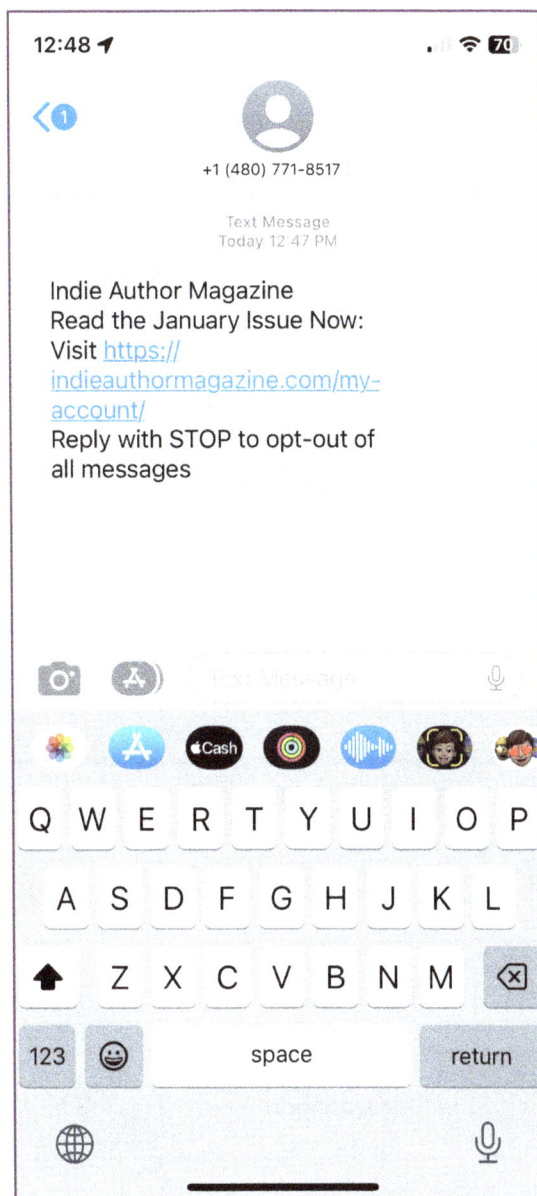

your work while also helping you create anticipation around your new releases.

Sendinblue also makes it easy for authors to manage their SMS campaigns with its automated system. You can easily schedule campaigns in advance and track performance using real-time analytics tools, so you know when messages are received and how many people have clicked on the links embedded in your text message.

Pro Tip: To ensure you've followed the proper laws regarding SMS permissions, ask subscribers to update their contact information with a phone number. Sendinblue has custom templates for updating preferences that can be added to the footer of emails, which can be shown alongside the required Unsubscribe link.

PRICING MODEL

There are two primary pricing models that email service providers use: pay-per-subscriber and pay-as-you-go. With monthly subscriptions, you pay a set amount each month with limits on the number of subscribers you can have. Some companies count subscribers even if they've unsubscribed, making it necessary to cull your lists often to ensure the account remains under the limits. Sendinblue, however, uses a pay-as-you-go model, which allows an unlimited number of subscribers and charges only for the number of emails sent.

PROVIDER	FREE PLAN	LOWEST PAID PLAN
Sendinblue	300 emails/day	$25/month for 40,000 emails
MailerLite	1,000 subscribers	$10/month for 1,000 subscribers
MailChimp	2,000 subscribers	$9.99/month for 500 subscribers
ActiveCampaign	14-day trial	$9/month for 500 contacts

The pay-as-you-go pricing model can be more cost-effective for authors that have a high number of inactive subscribers. With a pay-per-subscriber pricing model, businesses still have to pay for these inactive subscribers, even if they are not receiving any emails. With a pay-as-you-go pricing model, businesses only pay for the emails they send and not for subscribers who are not engaged.

For authors who use newsletter swap services, which can lead to extensive lists of prospects, a common complaint is they often bump up against sending limits according to their price tier. Sendinblue removes the need to ruthlessly remove contacts to keep from being charged a higher monthly fee.

Pro Tip: Import new subscribers to a prospects list, and send them a warm-up campaign. Invite them to join your main newsletter by clicking a button and using Sendinblue's marketing automation to move them to a validated list.

EMAIL AND LIST MANAGEMENT

List management is essential for authors looking to target their audience more effectively, and Sendinblue enables users to create, update, and manage multiple lists of subscribers. Sendinblue also provides the ability to import or export subscribers to and from different lists.

Sendinblue's personalized URLs (PURLs) feature allows users to capture contact information from multiple sources, such as web forms or landing pages, and store them in a list that you can segment later on. Segmentation allows authors to take advantage of dynamic content that Sendinblue automatically keeps track of when creating campaigns, such as the last time someone clicked and what they clicked on. Sendinblue lets you create segments based on various criteria such as subscriber activity, demographics, or behavior, tailoring your messages for each segment of your readership so that they feel special and engaged with your work.

Sendinblue also allows you to send automated campaigns based on specific criteria such as new subscribers, inactive subscribers, or those who have completed a purchase journey. This helps ensure readers receive timely messages that are tailored for them while keeping track of engagement levels with automated reports that show campaign performance.

Sendinblue also comes with other key features designed for advanced marketing:

Automation Based on Action: One of the most powerful features in Sendinblue is its ability to trigger emails based on certain user actions. Using this feature, authors can set up automated workflows and campaigns that send emails when users take specific actions, such as subscribing to their mailing list, visiting their website pages, or clicking on links in emails.

Personalization: Using Sendinblue's dynamic contact management tools, authors can personalize their emails using subscriber data, such as name, location, or purchase history. When readers feel like they have received an email tailored for them, they are more likely to open it and take action on it.

Advanced Targeting: Sendinblue also offers segmentation tools that allow you to target messages to specific segments of your readership based on criteria including activity level, such as those who have opened an email in the last thirty days; geography; demographics, such as gender or age; or the recency or frequency of past purchases, as well as other pieces of data.

Overall, Sendinblue is a unique option for self-published authors who are looking for a comprehensive digital marketing platform. With its email automation, SMS marketing, and chatbot integration, Sendinblue offers a range of tools that can help authors engage with their readers and promote their books. Additionally, its pricing is more affordable than many of its competitors, making it a great option for authors on a budget. ▪

Chelle Honiker

Tech Tools

Courtesy of IndieAuthorTools.com
Got a tool you love and want to share with us?
Submit a tool at IndieAuthorTools.com

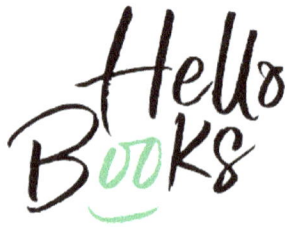	**HELLO BOOKS**	Hello Books is a new service that aims to help authors boost book sales and gain new readers. The platform offers a range of services including book cover design, ebook formatting, book trailers and book launch planning. It also allows authors to track their book's performance and analytics, and provides a dedicated account manager. https://hellobooks.com
	**BOOK-FUNNEL**	Bookfunnel is a service that assists authors in distributing their ebooks and audiobooks in a secure and professional manner. The platform offers a variety of features that assist authors in managing their book distribution and tracking the performance of their books including custom landing pages and facilitating cross-promotion. https://bookfunnel.com
	**STORY ORIGIN**	Storyorigin is a service designed to help authors promote their books and connect with readers. This platform offers a range of features that allow authors to create a professional author website, manage their book promotions and giveaways, and track their book's performance and analytics. https://storyoriginapp.com/
	**EMAIL LIST VALIDATION**	Email List Validation is a multi-level verification system that helps you clean up your email lists and increase deliverability. The pre-verification process weeds out disposable email addresses, spam, and address duplicates. With Email List Validation, you can save time and increase your email deliverability. https://appsumo.8odi.net/QOKqyM
	**BEEFREE.IO**	Beefree.io is a drag-and-drop email template builder that allows users to create and design professional-looking email campaigns without any coding experience. The platform integrates with popular email service providers such as MailChimp, Constant Contact, Campaign Monitor and more, which makes it easy to import and export templates and campaigns. https://beefree.io

Creative Connections

FOUR AUTHORS SHARE THE STORIES OF FRIENDSHIP THEY'VE PENNED THROUGH THEIR WRITING GROUPS

All writing groups are unique, yet they all share the ability to create deep bonds and lasting friendships among their members. In February, as we celebrate romantic relationships on Valentine's Day, we also want to celebrate the close-knit, creative relationships made in these spaces. *Indie Author Magazine* reached out to four writers to hear about their groups and what makes each of them so special.

A WORLD WIDE WEB OF INSPIRATION

Kate Baker lives and works on a farm in rural Suffolk, England. Her novel, *Maid of Steel*, a Historical Romance set in 1911 and 1912 New York and Queenstown, South Ireland, is set to publish with The Book Guild this month.

Because of her farm's location, it's difficult for Baker to be part of an in-person writing group, so instead she finds a home among those online. This makes her think of her "group" slightly differently. When asked, she writes she doesn't think about named spaces but about the personalities they contained. "I've

been a member of a few online writing groups in the last four years, and within each I've met people who inspire me to keep going [and] to write better," she writes.

When she began her writing journey in 2017, Baker joined her first writing group, The Fiction Cafe, on Facebook, where a friend introduced her to the Romantic Novelists Association. From there, she found out about Sophie Hannah's Dream Author coaching program (https://dreamauthorcoaching.com) and joined that space as well.

During this time Baker wrote her first novel—a novel now "lining the vegetable drawer," she jokes. However, she also discovered The Bestseller Experiment podcast and, after hearing their "encouraging noises about those who self-publish," joined their online academy. Through this, she met writers from all over the world and connected with them weekly via Zoom and daily via Facebook and dedicated chat boards.

Baker enjoys meeting writers in real life and attends away days and retreats when she is able—sometimes she bumps into people she's met online. However, recognizing the importance of forming deep, creative relationships, she admits that "to find some local writers would be the icing on the cake." Until this happens, Baker's support remains dispersed but strong nonetheless.

LIFELONG BONDS BUILT A WEEK AT A TIME

Lorraine Rogerson lives in Broadstairs, Kent, UK. She is writing a historical novel set in 1921 about a family unraveling after World War I. Rogerson has a master of arts in creative writing.

Rogerson met her writing group at an online workshop run by the Unthank School of Writing in 2016. Participants submitted two thousand words bi-weekly for the others to read and provide feedback on. For Rogerson, the workshop provided a level of accountability she needed. "We knew the characters in each other's novels inside-out before we even met each other," she writes. There were no Zoom calls at the time, so the group held "live" meetings in a Virtual Learning Environment. "Who knew that written chat … could be so quick-fire, so funny and so rewarding?" The group soon linked up on Facebook and began sharing tidbits from their wider reading and research ventures.

In 2017, three of the members finally met at a weeklong Thriller writing course run by Arvon.org at their center in Shropshire and had a tour of the newly refurbished Clockhouse writer's retreat. In 2018, all four returned for a long weekend. "[We] wrote, wrangled a bat, cooked and ate together and walked the grounds," she recalls. During those four days, the Clockhouse Chapter was formed.

In the Spring of 2019, the group returned for a full week. "I traveled straight from my mum's funeral, and couldn't have asked for a more nurturing, sympathetic and imaginative group to have been with," Rogerson writes. Evidence of the powerfully deep bonds that had been created could not be more clear.

Rogerson knows she owes a lot to the Clockhouse Chapter. "Writing brought us together and is still the focus of our friendship but there is so much more to it," she writes. Although they see each other regularly on Zoom, she's hoping that 2023 will be the year they go back to having a weeklong in-person retreat.

FRIENDSHIPS ROOTED IN WRITING

Robyn Sarty, of Belwood Publishing, has organized and published a series of fairy-tale retelling anthologies. She's a self-proclaimed lover of stories with happy endings and women who don't back down from a challenge—and her writing group's story may just fit the bill on both counts. "We're best friends as well as cheerleaders and sounding boards for each other," she writes. "[T]hese women have become some of the most important people in my life over the years we've known each other."

The seven writers first met in a National Novel Writing Month forum in March 2015, where they took part in a sandbox role-playing game together. At the July camp, Sarty and some of those she had met formed a private cabin so they could chat uninterrupted. And when the cabins closed in August, the group that had formed "stubbornly refused to reset their page," she writes. But eventually they needed a new home, and on Google Hangouts they chose the name "the Treehouse." In the years since, the group has migrated to Discord, where they're now known as the Treehouse of Writers. They still gather to "share writing and life struggles, funny memes, and … pictures of our fluffy writing companions," through a combination of written messages and a monthly Zoom catch-up call, Sarty writes.

Meeting in person is difficult with how far apart they all live from one another, but that doesn't put Sarty's group off. Over the years, they've organized in-person writing retreats and surprise visits with one another. Some even attended Sarty's wedding in 2016.

Support is a crucial part of the Treehouse ethic. When Sarty was suffering with depression and anxiety and using her writing as a distraction, she writes, her friends rallied around her. Her gratitude is evident. "Any time I need cheering up, I know they'll be there for me," she writes. "And I hope that I can do the same for them."

THE NEVER-ENDING FIVE-WEEK COURSE

Lisa Sergeant lives in South Cambridgeshire in the UK and writes weird and speculative fiction. She describes her current work in progress as "an American werewolf in London but with an Australian bunyip in Cambridge."

When Sergeant thinks of her writing group, the Mischievous Magpies, she thinks of seven friends who are "generous rather than competitive," and who she's "comfortable with however they might respond to my work."

The Magpies met during lockdown in 2020, when they signed up to a

bi-weekly online creative writing class. The initial five-week course was so successful, the teacher produced another, and then another. "The courses continue in the same format today," she writes, "so we continue to meet up on them every second Sunday."

Why are they called the Mischievous Magpies? The name came from a pin Sergeant found online with a magpie in the center and the words, "Work Hard, Stay Kind, Be Weird," around the edge. It summed up the group perfectly. "We laugh a lot when we're together and have supported each other not only through COVID but through other hard times as well, and mischievous was definitely the most appropriate collective noun," she writes.

Living in Cambridgeshire, Yorkshire, and Somerset, the Magpies don't meet up as much as they might like to. "We try to meet in person whenever an opportunity arises," Sergeant writes. "[T]hree of us have met at the Primadonna Festival, and there's been a book launch, and day trips where we've met half-way." They use WhatsApp to chat in the meantime.

There's a real warmth in her words about the group. "We're always in touch, reading each other's work, sharing links to writing courses and other opportunities, and of course recommending and talking about books, books, and more books," she writes. "The benefits are tremendous."

It doesn't matter who you are, where you live, or what you do—writing groups bring people together and strengthen into lasting relationships. This February, as we celebrate with our valentines, let's also celebrate our writing groups for enriching our lives in so many ways.

What is the story behind your writing group? How did you meet, and how has that relationship grown over time? Let us know at hello@ indieauthormagazine.com!

Jac Harmon

Podcasts We Love

Wish I'd Known Then... for Writers
Join authors Jami Albright and Sara Rosett as they interview self published authors about how they found success as well as what they've learned from their missteps. Because being an indie author is about being innovative and creative and learning from your mistakes.
https://wishidknownforwriters.com/

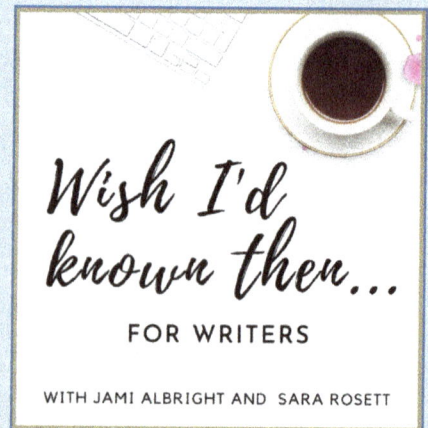

Wish I'd known then...
FOR WRITERS
WITH JAMI ALBRIGHT AND SARA ROSETT

Self-Publishing Authors
PODCAST
WWW.SPAGIRLSPODCAST.COM

SPA Girls
Each week the SPA Girls provide information, tips and honest advice on self publishing for indie authors. Hosted by four experienced self-publishing writers, we provide a mix of interviews, craft shows, and marketing information that will help you start your self-publishing journey.
https://www.selfpublishingauthorspodcast.com/

Creative Pep Talk
Hosted by Andy J. Pizza, a professional illustrator, speaker and author. The podcast aims to provide inspiration, practical advice and a dose of reality for creative entrepreneurs who want to build a career doing what they love. He covers a wide range of topics, including how to find your creative voice, how to handle creative blocks and rejection, and how to build a sustainable business. The show is aimed at artists, designers, writers and other creative professionals who want to build a career doing what they love, and is designed to provide inspiration, practical advice, and a dose of reality to help them achieve their goals.
https://podcasts.apple.com/us/podcast/creative-pep-talk/id929743897

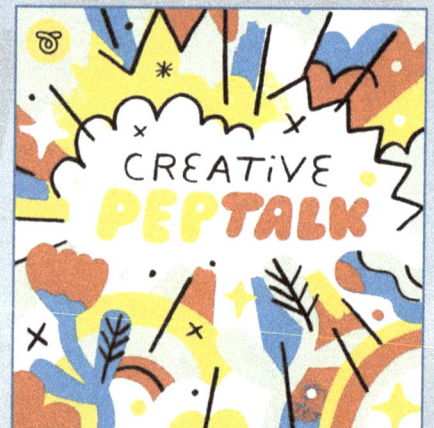

CREATIVE PEP TALK

Hello, My Name Is ...

WHY AUTHORS IN EVERY GENRE NEED TO CONSIDER THEIR CHARACTERS' NAMES CAREFULLY

A character's name can often make or break a book. How well would *Lord of the Rings* have gone over if it had followed Legolas, Gandalf, Aragorn, Gimli, Boromir, and their hobbit companions Bob and Doug McHobbit? Tolkien's editor might have had opinions. One imagines Kiki O'Hara would have also been quite a different character to Rhett Butler in *Gone with the Wind*.

It isn't just the accurate fit of a character's name in the genre that matters. Choosing a name for a character is a subtle art. It is a choice that can convey important details about a character's personality, background, and culture and may even alter the course of the character's arc—if that's something the writer chooses.

In Latin, "lector" translates to "one who reads." Given Dr. Hannibal Lector's penchant for studying his adversaries and gleaning their intentions, his name offers an entirely new, subtle menace to the character. *Stranger in a Strange Land* features a character named Jubal Harshaw, who becomes the de facto patriarch of the novel and its characters—almost a given, considering the name Jubal already refers to someone who is "Father of All." More recently, George R. R. Martin's *Game of Thrones*, both the novel and the show, feature the character Bran Stark, who is eventually referred to as "the three-eyed raven"—though with Bran being a Celtic word that means "raven," the character's fate was foreshadowed from the moment he was introduced.

Names can also have long-lasting, unintended effects. Donald Westlake, writing as Richard Stark, wrote a standalone crime novel starring a thief known only as Parker. This novel became a sixteen-book series, which Westlake lamented for a single reason. "It got tiresome after a while, trying to find some other way to say 'Parker parked the car.'" Imagine the sheer exhaustion Tolkien must have felt after spelling out a dozen Elvish names by hand during his writing.

Depending on the desired effect, a writer may choose a theme—such as Biblical or Greek names—to add depth to their characters. Plenty of resources exist to help writers find names in these categories and explore their underlying meanings. Behind the Name (http://behindthename.com) is an extensive database of names and their significance, with masculine, feminine, or cultural parameters that allow users to find options that may be suitable. For names that carry metaphorical significance, Nameberry (www.nameberry.com) is another helpful database of names and their meanings, also searchable by several parameters.

Whether we choose them for sentimental reasons, arcane reasons such as a hidden meaning or a veiled clue, or simply because we like the sound, we must consider the ramifications of the names we choose for our creations, no matter the genre or intent. The attention to detail can also be especially important for characters whose culture or ethnicity differs from your own—controversy surrounding the Harry Potter series' character Cho Chang, whose name is a mashup of two surnames from two different cultures, offers a perfect example as to why. Do our characters' names have to have subtext? Of course not. If a name fits your genre and you like the sound, by all means, put it to paper. But a carefully chosen name can give authors another method for adding an extra layer of depth to their worlds.

Just keep in mind that for all the subtle references or hidden meanings you might convey to your reader from your character's introduction, it's also possible to give away too much with a poorly chosen name. George Lucas, while never known for his subtlety, named his primary villain after the Dutch word for "father," spoiling one of his biggest plot twists for the series in the process—at least for those who spoke the language. Luckily, even a bad example can become an important lesson for a cautious writer: However you choose them, your characters' names make a difference. ◼

Eirynne Gallagher

Modern Love

WHY CONTEMPORARY ROMANCE REMAINS THE LEADING SUBGENRE

Boy meets girl. Boy loses girl. Boy gets girl back.

This simple formula for writing a romance is timeless, but Contemporary Romance puts a modern spin on these stories that makes them relevant for today's readers. Contemporary Romance reflects the issues, themes, problems, values, relationships, and lifestyle choices readers deal with in their own lives but guarantees one thing real life can't: a happily ever after (HEA).

WHAT IS CONTEMPORARY ROMANCE?

Romance Writers of America (RWA) characterizes <u>the Romance genre</u> as stories that have a "central love story and an emotionally satisfying ending." The tone, setting, and heat level may vary, but the defining element of a Contemporary Romance is that it is set after 1950 and focuses primarily on the relationship.

"Romance has always been popular," says Mark

Leslie Lefebvre, director of business development at Draft2Digital and a published author with more than a quarter century of experience in the bookselling industry. "In general, Romance is, by far, ten times bigger than any other genre in ebook publishing because Romance readers are the most voracious readers you'll ever find. They read faster. They read harder, and they read more consistently than any other readers."

Contemporary Romance is the <u>leading subgenre</u> within this category, according to Reedsy, a community that connects authors and freelance professionals.

But what's the appeal that keeps this Romance subgenre at the top of the list? Lorelei Buzzetta, a self-described "romance ambassador" and creative director of Lorelei's Lit Lair, a virtual Romance reader and author community, says it is all about the HEA. "The endings are always filled with love and hope … It satisfies the readers' expectations and fuels their love of reading."

CONTEMPORARY ROMANCE THEN AND NOW

Romance, as a genre, has its roots in eighteenth- and nineteenth-century fiction penned by authors such as Ann Radcliffe and Jane Austen. Over the decades, Romance novels, the subgenres, and the readership have evolved, but according to <u>Amanda Pagan, a children's librarian with the New York Public Library,</u> "historically, Romance novels separate themselves from other genres by being primarily written by women, for women, and about women."

That may have been true, even as recently as ten years ago, but male authors are moving in and making names for themselves in this female-dominated marketplace. Just ask Logan Chance, Mel Walker, and Rich Amooi, among others.

One hallmark of Contemporary Romance is that it reflects what's happening now—or what was happening then, for books published in years' past. Today's contemporary romantic fiction deals head-on with issues such as grief and loss (*Before I Let Go* by Kennedy Ryan), neurodiversity (*The Kiss Quotient* by Helen Hoang), multicultural relationships (*You Had Me at Hola* by Alexis Daria), and LGBTQ+ relationships (*Him* by Sarina Bowen).

Lefebvre says pop culture has a huge influence on the stories Contemporary Romance authors tell. The popularity of *Grey's Anatomy* led to an increase in medical romances. Ditto for *Sons of Anarchy*, which created demand for bad boy and motorcycle club romances, and *Fifty Shades of Grey*, which inspired the billionaire trend. Tuning into pop culture is one way authors can spot trends or hot topics to target themes, characters, and/or plots that may offer a strong hook to attract readers, such as royals and bachelors/insta-relationships, stemming from Harry and Meghan or today's plethora of reality dating shows, respectively.

USA Today bestselling Contemporary Romance author Melanie Harlow, first published in 2013, has released more than thirty titles. She's been on the forefront of changes to the genre but says there are some elements that remain consistent. "I think the structure of a romance—the bones of a good story—have remained unchanged. Those beats that readers expect—the meet-cute, the first kiss, the will-they-or-won't-they, the fun and games, the dark moment, the grovel—are all still there. Tropes endure as well. Enemies to lovers, second chance, friends to lovers, billionaires, the jilted bride. ... Those are evergreen and will always be popular."

As for changes in today's Contemporary Romance, Harlow shares these observations:

- a rise in popularity of dual first-person point of view
- authors choosing to distribute exclusively via Amazon's Kindle Unlimited to leverage page-read income versus wide distribution
- a shift from man-chest and couple covers to illustrated and discreet covers
- the impact of <u>#BookTok and TikTok</u> on book marketing thanks to viral posts and authors connecting with untapped readership
- an enhanced awareness of the value of tropes as marketing keywords but also in crafting a story that hits all the high notes for readers

TIPS FOR SUCCESS IN THE CONTEMPORARY ROMANCE MARKET

- **Study the Market:** Read the top sellers, data mine blurbs and ad copy, and track the tropes and trends.
- **Keep the Contract with Readers:** An HEA or HFN (happy for now) ending is non-negotiable.
- **Find a Niche You Love and Own It:** Consistency is key to building a solid readership.
- **Market to Reader Expectations:** Tropes not only help to craft a story that delivers on the promise to readers but can, and should, be part of marketing copy, such as book blurbs, to make buying decisions easier for readers who want a specific kind of book.
- **Focus on All the Feels for a Rich, Emotionally Satisfying Read:** Readers care about the characters and their journey to HEA.■

Maria Connor

Email Is the New Mailbox Money

When I was a young entrepreneur, the phrase "mailbox money" was thrown around a lot. I think, in today's world, email is the new mailbox money. When you do it effectively, it can be a source of income, either directly or indirectly. I think that's pretty cool.

If you're stuck or reluctant, you're not alone—that's for sure. But figuring out your email strategy shouldn't be something that holds you back from finding success as an author. Let's get you unstuck and some e-mailbox money headed your way.

Initially, I wasn't sure I'd have much to say about email and making money as a writer. This column, after all, is about the connection between prosperity and prose. But the more I thought about it, the more I realized there are a couple of delicious connections.

First, your email list is the only platform you own. Simultaneously, it's the only direct connection you have with your readers.

Second, procrastination seems to reign supreme when it comes to writers building their email lists.

If you don't believe you deserve to make money as a writer, chances are you won't find the courage to put yourself out there in another way in which you might fail.

Let's unpack this one nugget at a time, shall we? And I want to go in reverse.

It takes courage to put words onto paper (or screen). Without a strong sense of self and some serious self-confidence, negative feedback can temporarily trip us up or permanently shut us down. It stands to reason that if we're sure our writing won't stack up, we're not going to write the words.

That includes email words. Thus, procrastination.

Stack on top of that the unending drum beat of "build your email list!" complete with mixed messages about subject

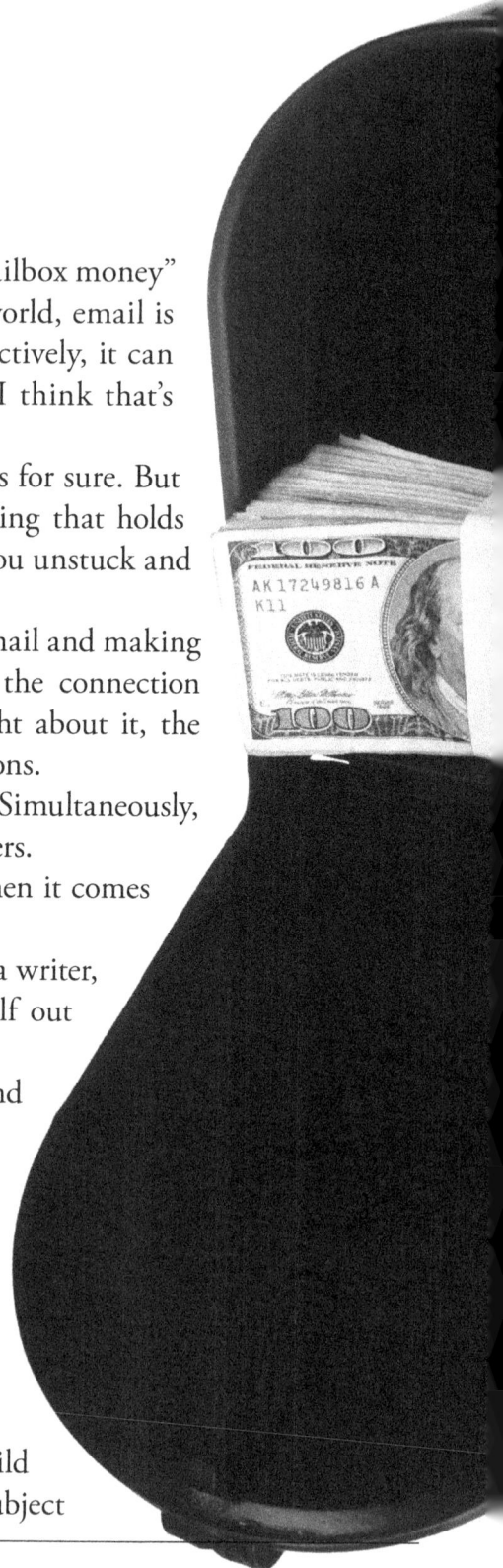

lines, length, and what works and what doesn't, and it is no wonder there's a temptation to just do it later.

Please allow me to help you break through any resistance or hesitation you have with a couple of quick thoughts and tips.

You can't do the wrong thing with the right person. You're in charge. You get to decide how much, how often, how long, and what you want to write about. Just today I received two emails: "THANK YOU for your emails this year! They have been so helpful!" and "Your emails are too long. Thomas Jefferson had a quote about that." I write for the former and ignore the latter. It's my email list, and they're my emails (in which I'm providing pretty awesome and free content, thanks so much). The folks my emails are for come and stay, and the other folks go fast (or eventually). Write what you want to write about, be yourself, and you'll be a magnet for readers—both of your emails and of your books.

You'll find your way as you find your way. I've had many iterations of my email strategies over the years. I've flipped from sending something every day to every couple of weeks to twice a week and back to almost every day. As long as I feel like I'm adding value and making a positive impact—and moving toward my goals and objectives—I keep going. And I do a regular check-in to make sure what I'm doing is working on all levels. You can too.

You know what to do. There's a lot of advice out there. Here's a bit more: Follow your gut, even as you're doing your research. I've gotten tons of advice that sounded right, but my instincts led me in a different direction. When I listened to my gut, I was right. Every time.

Here are a few suggestions to get you started:

- **Just start.** Confidence is created through action, so the more you do, the more you'll do. Decide what you want to write about and how often, and then just do it!
- **Your subscribers are grown adults.** The ones who want to stick around will stick around. Those who want to unsubscribe can do that. You do you! The more authentic you are, the more you'll attract the right folks to your list.
- **Iterate as desired.** If you start emailing on the first Tuesday of every month and then decide you like Fridays better, do that.

Remember—you're living the dream. You're writing for a living or moving in that direction. That's awesome. All successful authors, or at least all the ones I know, have email lists, so get started on yours, and pretty soon your e-mailbox money will be flowing! ■

Honorée Corder

Managing Your Author Career with Chronic Illness

If you're healthy and have never had a chronic illness, you're in a slim majority. According to the National Library of Medicine (https://www.ncbi.nlm.nih.gov), 45 percent of all Americans suffer from at least one chronic illness, and that doesn't include those with long COVID. If you don't suffer from a chronic illness, such as cancer, heart disease, or arthritis, chances are high that you may at some point in your life.

Roland Denzel sees the impact of chronic illness on writers every day. As a health coach and writer, he frequently advises those who want to live their best lives despite chronic illness. And although he does not suffer from a chronic illness himself, he works regularly with people who do.

For authors dealing with chronic illness, Denzel recommends thinking about their health as a funnel. You can only put so many things through a funnel at a time. Eventually, it will overflow. "There are things we can control, and there are things we can't," he says. "We don't know when a flare is going to come up."

The trick? Reduce the stressors within your control. Even things that are seemingly unrelated can still cause your funnel to overflow, such as poor sleep, overwork, or even relationship problems. "To our nervous system, all stress is virtually the same," he

A HEALTH COACH'S PERSPECTIVE

says. "It all has a big effect on us, whether it is directly related to our chronic illness or not."

Denzel has another unlikely tip for managing chronic illness: focusing on happiness. Previously obese and unhealthy, he, like many others, attempted to get his health back on track, but to no avail. "I had been tying my weight loss to my happiness, assuming that once I lost the weight, I would be happy."

That tie, it turned out, was the problem. When he focused exclusively on his happiness by faking it until it became a habit, his health improved: "I found a way to be happy, and I found a way to be healthy."

There is a link between happiness and chronic illness. According to a study by the Healthy Aging and Physical Rehabilitation Research and Training Center, or the RRTC (https://agerrtc.washington.edu), in which researchers surveyed over four hundred people with chronic illnesses, happier patients reported lower pain levels. Setting personal goals, engaging in spiritual activities, nurturing relationships, and expressing gratitude can be additional ways to find happiness, according to the RRTC.

"Find happiness" is easy advice to give but not so easy to do, especially when chronic illnesses can cause so much pain, but for Denzel, finding it is essential to better outcomes. "Our responsibility to the people around us is to not drag them down," Denzel says. "You have a responsibility to others to be happy for their sake, if not your own." ◾

Michael La Ronn

Romancing Your Readers

WHEN BUILDING A RELATIONSHIP WITH YOUR FANS, IT'S OK TO SHARE ABOUT LIFE BEYOND YOUR BOOKS

Authors everywhere want fans to love and purchase their books. We spend every day marketing our books to readers and potential readers, but sometimes we forget we need to market ourselves to our readers as well.

Fans want to get to know the person behind the pen. When fans feel like they have a personal connection to you as an author, they are more likely to be invested in you and, subsequently, your books. In return, you'll be able to create a loyal following that buys every release and promotes your books.

So how do you build a personal connection with your fans?

You must romance them, and the best way to do that is to be honest.

Even though we all want to keep a certain level of privacy in our lives, we should allow our fans to get a little insight into who we are without sharing too much. Think of it like a first date, but with your readers. They want to get to know you better. Do you have pets? Do you go for walks in the morning or evening? Do you have a hobby outside of writing? Are you willing to share a picture of your writing workspace? How about a video of yourself while you write?

Sharing snapshots from your personal life is an easy way to create a personal connection with readers. You may worry that your life is boring and your readers won't be interested in it, but even things that are mundane for authors, like writing or editing, could be interesting for your readers. You could even share a funny typo that totally changed a sentence's meaning. Readers will laugh alongside you.

If you have a hobby you like to talk about, you can ask your fans about their hobbies and to share pictures of their hobbies with you. The same works for pets. People love to share pictures of their pets, and if you ask them to share a recent picture of their pets, many of them will do so. This gets them to interact with you, and they'll continue to do so as they see more posts from you.

If you aren't comfortable sharing pictures of yourself often, of course, you don't have to. As you build up confidence in sharing pictures of other things in your world, you'll eventually find you're willing to share pictures of yourself and what you are doing. You'll be surprised how many comments you'll get on your pictures from your fans. And if pictures really aren't your thing, you could write about things going on in your daily life instead.

As you develop a closer relationship with your readers over time, you will be surprised by how many fans will send you random notes of encouragement, small gifts when you've been sick, or just something out of the blue to brighten your day.

Take a chance and share something about your personal life with your readers, and see how they react! You may just find it gives you a little boost of dopamine and improves your day— and theirs. ■

Grace Snoke

Buying Back Your Time

IS IT TIME TO HIRE OUTSIDE HELP TO KEEP YOUR AUTHOR BUSINESS RUNNING?

If only we really could buy time back when we needed it, life as an author would be so much easier. Sadly, we're still stuck with twenty-four hours in a day, like everyone else. And, of course, we don't want to spend our lives either literally working 24/7 or feeling like we do. We all need breaks away from what we're doing. We all need time to switch off and enjoy life.

Just as importantly, when we are working on our author business, we want to be doing the best we can with what we've got. And that means working on the things we personally need to be doing.

If you want to grow your author business, at some point, you will have to hand over some of your tasks to other people who can help. More than that, you may well be dying to do that just because you'll feel happier. Think of the tasks you really hate doing in your author business, whether it's updating your back matter, writing your newsletter, or managing paid ads.

The problem with tasks that you really don't want to do isn't just the time it takes to do them; it's the time you spend dreading doing them, putting them off, and tootling around on Facebook because you can't face your to-do list. If you add up all of that time lost over an entire year, it's probably hours that you could have spent doing the things that move the needle in your author business.

But what can you delegate? How do you do it? What does it cost? There are a lot of questions when it comes to delegating parts of your business, and we'll cover what you need to know to get started in this article.

WHERE DO YOU START?

When deciding what to delegate, it's best to start with making a list of the things only you can do.

Think about how you run your author business and look at the tasks you do regularly. Which ones really have to be done by you and no one else? Unless you want to use a ghostwriter for your books, number one on your list is probably writing. What else on your to-do list drives your business forward or supports you financially? Those are the things you should focus your energy on the most.

Once you have that down, make a list of the tasks you could outsource in order to free up the most time. On this list, include anything that you dread doing, anything that people with the right expertise can do better and quicker than you, and anything that will save you noticeable amounts of time that you can put to better use.

Unless you're already in a great financial position, you'll likely find that you have more things you'd like to delegate than budget to do so. Your next step is to prioritize and decide which tasks will make the biggest difference to you that you can currently afford.

After that, you're ready to start looking for the right people to help you take your author business forward.

WHAT CAN YOU DELEGATE?

Handing parts of your author business over to someone else shouldn't be worrisome. In fact, chances are you're already doing that. Most authors don't do their own book covers or editing. You likely have an accountant or a bookkeeper to help with your taxes. You've probably paid for a newsletter builder or to get your book promoted by a site like Freebooksy or Robin Reads. You're already taking advantage of someone else's skills and knowledge to gain something for your author business in exchange for money. That is delegating. But you can apply the principle to far more.

Many authors have one or more virtual assistants to help them get beta readers, manage their ARC teams, run their Facebook groups, create promo graphics, send out their newsletter, and more. You can pay people to do pretty much any aspect of your author business for you, including plot generation, marketing, editing, formatting, newsletter swaps, website design, social media management, selling your books directly, and uploading your books to the various publishing platforms.

The business side of things is sorted, but we're not done yet. What about at home? Do you really love cleaning all that much? What about laundry, cooking, or the list of honey-dos that you've said for months that you'd get around to doing eventually? Yes, those things are a part of life, but if you have the budget and they're getting in the way of you getting the words down, then it might be worthwhile to consider outsourcing home tasks as well.

But how much does it all cost?

There are too many tasks that you could outsource for us to give you a definitive list, but outsourcing can cost less than you think.

Virtual assistants can start as low as around ten dollars an hour according to a quick look at different VA pages on Facebook, but experienced business managers can also charge as high as five- or six-figure full-time salaries to run everything for you. Delegated, a VA hiring platform, offers an in-depth look at rates and provides some hiring tips (https://delegated.com/resources/virtual-assistant-cost-calculator). Costs can be even less if you delegate to somewhere like the Philippines, where rates are far lower.

Pro Tip: You will need to manage time differences, but depending on where you live, you may be able to save by using an assistant from a different country. For example, if you live in the UK and hire a US assistant that bills at ten dollars per hour, you'll actually pay around eight pounds an hour (variable depending on the current exchange rate), compared to hiring a UK assistant who charges ten pounds an hour.

Formatters, editors, cover designers—all of these necessary author helpers have a whole range of prices. Our advice? Do your research, look at examples of their work and testimonials, then buy the best you can afford right now without breaking your budget or getting yourself into trouble. You can always upgrade to better covers or formatting, or outsource more tasks, when you have a bigger budget down the road.

Pro Tip: Where can you find a great VA? Our best advice is to ask other authors and get recommendations. You can also search for Facebook groups that connect authors with assistants. Or you could try sites such as Fiverr, Upwork, and People per Hour, though we stress the need to do your research and perhaps start with a trial project.

CAN YOU STILL DELEGATE IF YOU HAVE NO BUDGET?

The short answer is "yes." There are various author groups on Facebook where you can advertise for what you need. You can get lucky and find someone who'd love to help in exchange for free books. You might be able to swap skills with another author to get what you need. Newer virtual assistants may provide free or lower cost help for a certain period of time in exchange for testimonials or reviews. You may even find that a fan would love to help just because they like you.

You really don't have to wait. With a bit of creativity, you can find ways to hand off at least some things from your to-do list.

THINGS TO THINK ABOUT

Naturally, there's going to be a learning curve with new hires. When you're used to doing everything on your own, it can be hard to let someone else manage things for you. You'll need to spend time training your new people on what you want and how you want them to do things.

For a while, you might feel like you have more on your plate, but as your new helpers start to learn the ropes, you'll find that suddenly you have more time to write and more mental space to relax.

The other thing to consider is that you may be handing over sensitive information about your business to someone else, so you have to be sure that you've done your research and chosen the right person. For example, you'll need to provide confidential financial and business information to anyone working as your bookkeeper, accountant, or lawyer, so take your time choosing those people.

Think about security. Depending on their roles, your new hires may need to have access to your KDP and Draft2Digital dashboards, and you don't want to give those to just anyone. Luckily, software, such as LastPass (https://lastpass.com/), will let you share access without revealing your username and password. AVirtual also has an excellent article on maintaining security in these situations: https://avirtual.co.uk/2018/11/16/share-private-data-with-virtual-pa/.

Take up references, interview potential new hires in person or on Zoom, and get to know them before you get started. You'll be spending a lot of time with this person, especially at first, and you need to be sure you'll get along. Perhaps start off with just one task or a short-term hire to see how things go before bringing someone new on full time, and don't be afraid to let someone go if it's not working out. This is your

business, and you're building a team that has to work for you.

Also cover yourself with a contract, whether that's between you and the site, if you use something like TaskRabbit (https://taskrabbit.com), or you and your new hire. Specify terms and conditions, pay, hours and tasks, notice period, if applicable, and everything else you want to cover to make sure everything is spelled out should anything go wrong. It's likely that your virtual assistant will already have a standard contract, but if not, We Are Indy has a helpful sample contract and information on what should be included (https://weareindy.com/blog/a-guide-to-virtual-assistant-contracts-and-templates).

Although you might not be able to delegate everything you'd like immediately, you can start small and get there over time. Delegate what you can, then use the time and mental space you've freed up to build your business so that you're making more money and spending time doing those things that make your heart truly sing: writing, spending time with your family and friends, actually having weekends, and having the room and freedom to have time off when you need the break.

Delegating means knowing that your author business will keep powering along nicely with the team that you built to keep it going, even when you aren't there. Is that worth the cost? We say definitely. ◼

Gill Fernley

From the Stacks

Courtesy of IndieAuthorTools.com
Got a book you love and want to share with us?
Submit a book at IndieAuthorTools.com

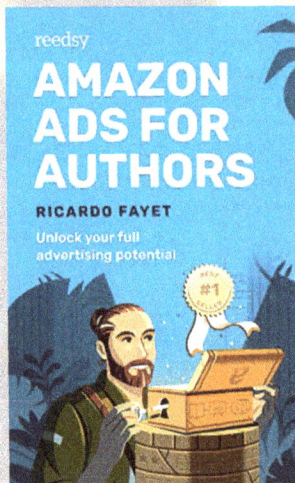

Amazon Ads for Authors: Unlock Your Full Advertising Potential

Ricardo Fayet

Amazon Ads for Authors aims to help authors run profitable advertising campaigns on Amazon. Written by Ricardo Fayet, Co-founder of Reedsy, who has helped hundreds of authors with their Amazon ads and managed over a million dollars in advertising spend. The book is the second of the popular Reedsy Marketing Guides series. The book covers the fundamental guiding principles of advertising books on Amazon, how to build a comprehensive list of product and keyword targets, what type of ad campaign will best suit your book, how to optimize your click-through-rate to boost delivery, how to optimize your campaigns for profit and how to scale and progressively grow your spend while keeping your profit levels. Each step is illustrated with examples and screenshots for easy understanding and application. This book is suitable for authors who are just starting with Amazon Advertising or have been running ads for years.

https://books2read.com/u/3JojLK

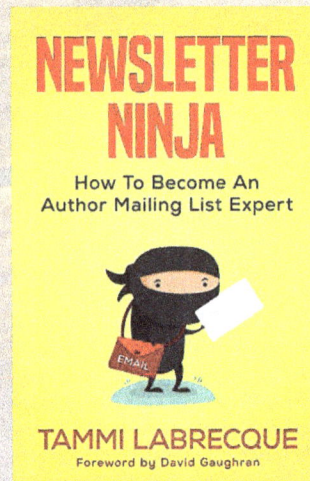

Newsletter Ninja

Tammi Labrecque

"Newsletter Ninja" is a comprehensive resource that teaches authors how to build and maintain a strongly engaged email list. The book offers new ways to think about your email list, re-energize existing subscribers, embrace next level methods and improve engagement. Authors can use the book to build a list of passionate readers, and launch their books into the charts. The author also covers open rates, click rates, and engagement, and teaches authors about themselves, their readers, and what they're really selling when they email. This book is aimed at authors who are building a mailing list, want to grow an existing one or simply want to raise their email game.

https://books2read.com/u/bONxjQ

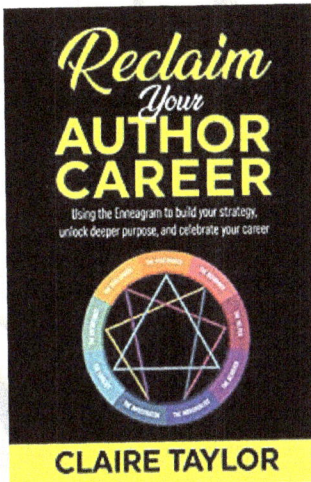

Reclaim Your Author Career: Using the Enneagram to build your strategy, unlock deeper purpose, and celebrate your career Kindle Edition

Claire Taylor

Reclaim Your Author Career is a book that provides a simple framework to align an author's business and career. Written by bestselling author and story consultant Claire Taylor, the book is aimed at indie authors who are struggling to stay in the game and are looking to supercharge their career while staying true to their values. The book uses the Enneagram framework to help writers rediscover their core motivation and align their work with what fuels them. By examining creative values, persona, themes, and protagonists, the author guides readers through an exploration of themselves that will leave them wiser, refreshed, and excited to make the tough decisions that lead to lasting success. The book covers topics such as identifying distractions and stressors that lead you off course, attracting the right readers for your books, leveraging theme to build your fandom, and why picking the right protagonist can make or break your brand. It is an insightful guide to build a writing life that fits, brings satisfaction, and empowers to create a life worth celebrating.
https://books2read.com/u/bxrn9q

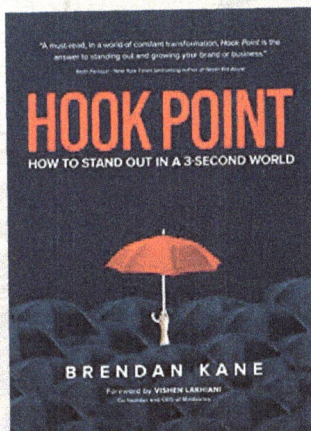

Hook Point: How to Stand Out in a 3-Second World Kindle Edition

Brendan Kane

Hook Point: How to Stand Out in a 3-Second World is a book by out-of-the-box thinker Brendan Kane that provides strategies for generating new opportunities, innovating and scaling businesses, and creating compelling brands in today's micro-attention world. The book addresses the challenges that brands and individuals face in grabbing the attention of potential audiences in a world where digital and social media have reshaped communication and marketing. With an average of over sixty billion messages shared on digital platforms each day and an average person exposed to between four thousand to ten thousand ads a day, Kane argues that we have less than three seconds to capture a person's attention. He introduces the concept of "hook points," a communication tool that helps marketers package their messages in a succinct, attention-grabbing way that leads to better opportunities both online and off. The book is intended as an essential guide for promoting a brand, product, or service in today's fast-paced and crowded digital world.
https://books2read.com/u/3nDWqK

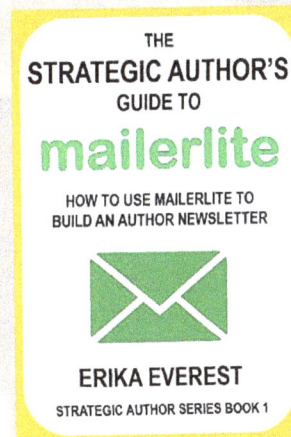

The Strategic Author's Guide to MailerLite: How to use MailerLite to build an author newsletter

Erika Everest

The Strategic Author's Guide to MailerLite provides a step-by-step guide on how to build an author newsletter from scratch, using the popular mailing list provider MailerLite. The book is intended for authors who are struggling to get started with newsletters, overwhelmed by the learning curve, know what they want but not how to achieve it, or find managing their list taking too much of their time. The book covers topics such as how to prioritize marketing efforts by tracking where subscribers see you, free up time and create superfans with a set-and-forget onboarding sequence, save time and increase brand strength with email templates, build rapport with readers even before books are published, and use step-by-step timesavers to get your newsletter going painlessly. The book is designed to help authors spend their time and money in ways that will give them the biggest result for their efforts, and shows them how to establish a newsletter to sell more books.
https://books2read.com/u/47VXvE

In This Issue

Executive Team

Chelle Honiker, Publisher

As the publisher of Indie Author Magazine, Chelle Honiker brings nearly three decades of startup, technology, training, and executive leadership experience to the role. She's a serial entrepreneur, founding and selling multiple successful companies including a training development company, travel agency, website design and hosting firm, a digital marketing consultancy, and a wedding planning firm. She's organized and curated multiple TEDx events and hired to assist other nonprofit organizations as a fractional executive, including The Travel Institute and The Freelance Association.

As a writer, speaker, and trainer she believes in the power of words and their ability to heal, inspire, incite, and motivate. Her greatest inspiration is her daughters, Kelsea and Cathryn, who tolerate her tendency to run away from home to play with her friends around the world for months at a time. It's said she could run a small country with just the contents of her backpack.

Alice Briggs, Creative Director

As the creative director of Indie Author Magazine, Alice Briggs utilizes her more than three decades of artistic exploration and expression, business startup adventures, and leadership skills. A serial entrepreneur, she has started several successful businesses. She brings her experience in creative direction, magazine layout and design, and graphic design in and outside of the indie author community to her role.

With a masters of science in Occupational Therapy, she has a broad skill set and uses it to assist others in achieving their desired goals. As a writer, teacher, healer, and artist, she loves to see people accomplish all they desire. She's excited to see how IAM will encourage many authors to succeed in whatever way they choose. She hopes to meet many of you in various places around the world once her passport is back in use.

Nicole Schroeder, Editor in Chief

Nicole Schroeder is a storyteller at heart. As the editor in chief of Indie Author Magazine, she brings nearly a decade of journalism and editorial experience to the publication, delighting in any opportunity to tell true stories and help others do the same. She holds a bachelor's degree from the Missouri School of Journalism and minors in English and Spanish. Her previous work includes editorial roles at local publications, and she's helped edit and produce numerous fiction and nonfiction books, including a Holocaust survivor's memoir, alongside independent publishers. Her own creative writing has been published in national literary magazines. When she's not at her writing desk, Nicole is usually in the saddle, cuddling her guinea pigs, or spending time with family. She loves any excuse to talk about Marvel movies and considers National Novel Writing Month its own holiday.

Monthly Columnists

Honorée Corder

Honorée Corder is the author of more than fifty books, an empire builder, and encourager of writers. When she's not writing, she's spoiling her dog and two cats, eating something fabulous her husband made on the grill, working out, or reading. She hopes this article made a positive impact on your life, and if it did, you'll reach out to her via Honoree-Corder.com.

Craig Martelle

High school Valedictorian enlists in the Marine Corps under a guaranteed tank contract. An inauspicious start that was quickly superseded by excelling in language study. Contract waived, a year at the Defense Language Institute to learn Russian and off to keep my ears on the big red machine during the Soviet years. Earned a four-year degree in two years by majoring in Russian Language. My general staff. career included choice side gigs – UAE, Bahrain, Korea, Russia, and Ukraine.

Major Martelle. I retired from the Marines after a couple years at the embassy in Moscow working arms control issues.

Department of Homeland Security then law school next. I was working for a high-end consulting firm performing business diagnostics, business law, and leadership coaching. For the money they paid me, I was good with that. Just until I wasn't. Then I started writing.

Writers

Angela Archer

Having worked as a mental health nurse for many years, Angela combines her love of words with her love of human psychology to work as a copywriter in the UK. She independently published a novella and novel in 2020 and is currently fending off the lure of shiny new novel ideas to complete the second book in her sci-fi series. When she's not tinkering with words, she's usually drinking tea, playing the saxophone (badly), or being mum and wife to her husband and two boys.

Maria Connor

Maria Connor is the founder and owner of My Author Concierge, which provides high-level project management support services to self-published authors, She is the author of The Self-Publishing Checklist Series, a USA Today bestselling contemporary romance author, and an international speaker on writing, editing, marketing, and publishing topics. Since 2010, she has worked with more than a hundred authors across all genres, published more than 35 titles herself, and presented more than 30 workshops regionally, nationally, and internationally.

Gill Fernley

Gill Fernley writes fiction in several genres under different pen names, but what all of them have in common is humor and romance, because she can't resist a happy ending or a good laugh. She's also a freelance content writer and has been running her own business since 2013. Before that, she was a technical author and documentation manager for an engineering company and can describe to you more than you'd ever wish to know about airflow and filtration in downflow booths. Still awake? Wow, that's a first! Anyway, that experience taught her how to explain complex things in straightforward language and she hopes it will come in handy for writing articles for IAM. Outside of writing, she's a cake decorator, expert shoe hoarder, and is fluent in English, dry humor and procrastibaking.

Eirynne Gallagher

Eirynne J Gallagher is an Austin, Texas transplant. She holds a BA and MA in English and Creative Writing. Her short fiction has appeared in Analog Science Fiction & Fact and Ares Magazine. Her novels are available at most online retailers.

Jac Harmon

While studying for her doctorate in Medieval History Jac Harmon spent her time poking around in old buildings and reading manuscripts which gave her plenty of experience when it came to doing the research for her historical fiction. After many years spent working in university administration herding students she is now getting involved in voluntary work at a historic house and being trained in paper conservation. The idea behind this being that one day she'll be allowed to get her hands on some of the rare books in the library

there. Not that this will help with her current novel which is set in the seedy criminal underworld of late-Victorian London. An era of gas lights and grime which was purposefully chosen to give her an excuse to indulge in her love of all things Gothic. Dark twists and bad weather are to be expected.

Michael La Ronn

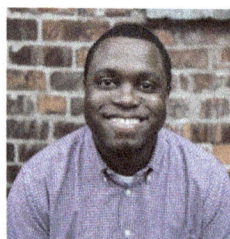

Michael La Ronn has published over 80 science fiction & fantasy books and self-help books for writers. He built a writing career publishing 10-12 books per year while raising a family, working a full-time job, and even attending law school classes in the evenings. He is also the Outreach Manager at the Alliance of Independent Authors, a nonprofit organization for self-published writers. Visit his fiction website at www.michaellaronn.com and his resources for writers at www.authorlevelup.com.

Megan Linski-Fox

Megan Linski lives in Michigan. She is a USA TODAY Bestselling Author and the author of more than fifty novels. She has over fifteen years of experience writing books alongside working as a journalist and editor. She graduated from the University of Iowa, where she studied Creative Writing.

Grace Snoke

Grace Snoke is a 42-year-old author and personal assistant residing in Lincoln, Nebraska. Having been a corporate journalist for more than a decade and a video game journalist for even longer, writing has been something she has always enjoyed doing. In addition to non-fiction books, she is currently working on a paranormal romance series, and two urban fantasy series under her real name. She has also released more than a dozen illustrated children's books and several non-fiction books. She has been publishing erotica under a pen name since 2017. For more information about her personal assistant business visit: https://spiderwebzdesign.net. Her author site is: https://gracesnoke.com.

Wendy Van Camp

Wendy Van Camp is the Poet Laureate for the City of Anaheim, California. Her work is influenced by cutting edge technology, astronomy, and daydreams. A graduate of the Ad Astra Speculative Fiction Workshop, Wendy is a nominated finalist for the Elgin Award, for the Pushcart Prize, and for a Dwarf Stars Award. Her poems, stories, and articles have appeared in: "Starlight Scifaiku Review", "The Junction", "Quantum Visions", and other literary journals. She is the poet and illustrator of "The Planets: a scifaiku poetry collection" and editor of the annual anthology "Eccentric Orbits: An Anthology of Science Fiction Poetry". Find her at https://wendy-vancamp.com

Ready to level up your indie author career?

Trick question. Of course you are.

*INDIE ^Author Tools

Get Your Friday Five Newsletter and find your next favorite tool here.

https://writelink.to/iat

Join the Facebook group here.

https://writelink.to/iatfb

www.ingramcontent.com/pod-product-compliance
Lightning Source LLC
Chambersburg PA
CBHW081747200326
41597CB00024B/4423